THE
POWER
—— OF ——
EMPLOYEE
WELL-BEING

THE
POWER
—— OF ——
EMPLOYEE
WELL-BEING

MOVE BEYOND ENGAGEMENT
TO BUILD FLOURISHING TEAMS

MARK C. CROWLEY

BK

Berrett–Koehler Publishers, Inc.

Berrett-Koehler Publishers, Inc.
1333 Broadway, Suite P100
Oakland, CA 94612-1921
Tel: (510) 817-2277
Fax: (510) 817-2278
bkconnection.com

ORDERING INFORMATION
Quantity sales. Special discounts are available on quantity purchases by corporations, associations, and others. For details, please go to bkconnection.com to see our bulk discounts or contact bookorders@bkpub.com for more information.

Individual sales. Berrett-Koehler publications are available through most bookstores. They can also be ordered directly from Berrett-Koehler: Tel: (800) 929-2929; Fax: (802) 864-7626; bkconnection.com.

Orders for college textbook / course adoption use. Please contact Berrett-Koehler: Tel: (800) 929-2929; Fax: (802) 864-7626.

Distributed to the US trade and internationally by Penguin Random House Publisher Services.

The authorized representative in the EU for product safety and compliance is EU Compliance Partner, Pärnu mnt. 139b-14, 11317 Tallinn, Estonia, www.eucompliancepartner.com, +372 5368 65 02.

Berrett-Koehler and the BK logo are registered trademarks of Berrett-Koehler Publishers, Inc.

Printed in the United State of America

Berrett-Koehler books are printed on long-lasting acid-free paper. When it is available, we choose paper that has been manufactured by environmentally responsible processes. These may include using trees grown in sustainable forests, incorporating recycled paper, minimizing chlorine in bleaching, or recycling the energy produced at the paper mill.

Cataloging-in-Publication Data is on file at the Library of Congress.
Library of Congress Control Number: 2025007690
ISBN 9798890571298 (hardcover) | ISBN 9798890571304 (pdf) |
ISBN 9798890571311 (epub)

First Edition

33 32 31 30 29 28 27 26 25   10 9 8 7 6 5 4 3 2 1

Book production: Happenstance Type-O-Rama
Jacket design: Ashley Ingram
Author photo: Ted Wittman

CONTENTS

FOREWORD

In today's fast-paced business world, one truth has become undeniable: traditional employee engagement surveys just don't cut it anymore. The questions may have changed over the years, but the premise remains the same—and it's outdated. What's missing is a deeper, more human approach that prioritizes what really matters: employee well-being.

This is exactly where Mark C. Crowley's *The Power of Employee Well-Being* steps in. Mark invites us to shift our focus from chasing engagement scores to understanding what it takes for people to genuinely thrive. Backed by groundbreaking research—including data from the University of Oxford's study of over twenty million workers—he shows how well-being isn't just a feel-good buzzword; it's a driver of performance and productivity. When employees feel valued, supported, and emotionally connected to their work, their potential knows no bounds.

Mark's ideas aren't just insightful; they're actionable. Building on the foundation of his bestselling book, *Lead from the Heart*, he delivers a clear, compelling road map for leaders. What I admire most is how practical this book is. The short, focused chapters make it easy for busy managers to quickly absorb new information and to put it to immediate use. In a world where time is one of our most precious resources, this design is a gift.

Over my career, I've worked with countless executives and organizations, and I can tell you this: the way forward is clear. It's not about squeezing out another percentage point on an engagement survey. It's about truly investing in the well-being of your people—and reaping the extraordinary benefits that follow. This book gives you the tools and strategies to make that happen.

Mark doesn't just offer a new way of thinking; he's calling for a fundamental shift in how we lead. For organizations ready to embrace this change, *The Power of Employee Well-Being* is the guide you've been waiting for. It's time to stop settling for outdated metrics and start focusing on what really matters—creating workplaces where people flourish and organizations soar.

—DR. MARSHALL GOLDSMITH, Thinkers50 #1 Executive
Coach and *New York Times* bestselling author of *The Earned Life*, *Triggers*, and *What Got You Here Won't Get You There*

THE
POWER
—— OF ——
EMPLOYEE
WELL-BEING

INTRODUCTION

Don't Measure Engagement—
Support Employee Well-Being Instead

The well-being of your employees
directly impacts the well-being of your company.

—DOUG CONANT,
former President of Nabisco and
former CEO of Campbell's Soup[1]

In 2013, *Fast Company* was first to announce the findings of Gallup's massive State of the American Workplace study.[2] The researchers' stunning discovery at the time was that only 30 percent of US workers were fully engaged in their jobs—meaning just one in three employees were willing to invest discretionary effort into helping their organizations succeed. (Gallup would later report that engagement scores were even worse in Europe and the UK.[3])

In a sense, this alarming announcement was a shot heard 'round the world in business. Gallup found that more than half of workers were doing just enough work to collect a paycheck, and nearly one in five were so unhappy in their jobs that they had become "actively disengaged"— vengeful saboteurs acting out their dissatisfaction through negative behavior.

Because such a significant majority of employees proved to be emotionally disconnected from their workplaces—and inherently not giving their best efforts at work—Gallup's key conclusion was that poor engagement was severely undermining organizational productivity, driving up costs for businesses and urgently requiring a remedy.

For two decades now, "engagement" has been a buzzword in our workplaces. Hundreds of books have been written on this topic, all promising that a commitment to improving engagement would result in lower turnover rates, superior employee morale, and enhanced overall performance.

And considering the massive upside that existed for companies were they to win back a greater percentage of their employees' hearts and minds, one might imagine that major initiatives were launched everywhere, leading to a significant improvement in engagement scores.

Remarkably, that's not what happened at all.

Employee engagement in America today remains stagnant at around 31 percent—essentially unchanged since 2013.[4] Globally, the picture is even worse: Gallup estimates that just 21 percent of employees worldwide are engaged.[5]

Why Engagement Never Improved

I asked a large and varied group of workplace leaders why they believed engagement had failed to become a major priority in their companies, and the responses proved highly consistent.

Most stressed that investors never held CEOs accountable for engagement because other well-established metrics for evaluating organizational performance were deemed more important. On top of that, employees were generally surveyed no more than twice a year. It often took months for the results to be distributed to managers, and poor scores were never assigned to a specific person to fix. Rarely were managers' performance reviews or compensation tied to improving engagement. Ultimately, the workers themselves grew to believe the survey process was a complete joke, leading many to conclude that their employers didn't really care about their feelings and concerns at all. Ironically, this perceived indifference led people to become even *less* engaged in their jobs.

While it's well known that some companies—including Google, Microsoft, Salesforce, Patagonia, Zappos, and others—took employee engagement very seriously and committed themselves to being great places to work, time has shown that the vast majority of organizations simply went on to treat engagement as a tick-the-box exercise rather than demonstrating any genuine commitment to improving their workplaces.

And as they were never held responsible for elevating engagement within their own teams, most managers came to consider it to be HR's job, rather than an integral part of their own core leadership responsibilities.

It's Time to Move on from Employee Engagement: Poor Well-Being Is the Real Threat to Organizational Performance

For over two decades,[6] chasing employee engagement has largely been all talk and no action. So, going forward, it's time for leaders to stop focusing on what has really become a meaningless metric and to instead focus on one that actually matters: employee well-being.

As an important distinction, efforts to improve employee engagement aim at motivating workers to become more committed to their companies and jobs, while efforts to improve well-being focus on enhancing employees' overall health and happiness. An intentional pivot toward elevating well-being will help solve two rather significant problems facing businesses today.

The first of these problems is that chronic employee burnout has become an epidemic, leading to costly turnover. One Deloitte study found that 77 percent of US professionals have experienced burnout at their current job, with 91 percent saying that having an unmanageable amount of stress and exhaustion negatively impacts the quality of their work.[7] As a result, an astonishing one in five American workers reportedly have *daily* thoughts about quitting their jobs.[8]

The second problem facing organizations today is that managers are so incentivized to meet their targets that they're not effectively supporting their employees' emotional and psychological needs. A report from employment and labor law company Littler found a 74 percent surge in employees requesting leave or accommodations for mental health–related issues in just one year, from 2023 to 2024.[9]

There is also mounting evidence that improving their sense of well-being at work has become a personal priority for most people,[10] with 84 percent of respondents to a separate Deloitte survey identifying this as their number one priority—even more important to them than getting ahead in their careers.[11]

As punctuation, the American Psychological Association's 2023 Work in America survey found that 92 percent of workers consider it very or somewhat important to work for an organization that demonstrates it values their emotional and psychological well-being.[12]

The pursuit of well-being also had a direct impact on employee retention in the months after offices reopened following the COVID-19 pandemic lockdowns. Between January 2021 and June 2023, there was an unprecedented spike in the number of American workers who quit their jobs each month, with approximately 20 percent of the workforce leaving a job in 2021 alone. This astonishing mass exodus, now widely known as the "Great Resignation," was driven by factors such as low pay, feeling disrespected, a lack of opportunities for advancement, and *the desire for better work-life balance and well-being.*[13]

All of this data not only signals that employee well-being is in great peril, but also implies that to ensure their organizations retain their talent, leaders must quickly pivot in ways that will ensure their employees thrive.

Insights from the World's Largest Well-Being Study

Oxford University Saïd Business School professor Jan-Emmanuel De Neve partnered with global employment firm Indeed and asked website visitors to anonymously grade their responses to four questions:

1. Do you feel happy most of the time?

2. Are you content with your work?

3. Do you find your work to be purposeful and worthwhile?

4. Are you experiencing negative stress at work?

Remarkably, as of 2025, over 20 million people had submitted responses, making it one of the largest studies on work happiness ever performed.[14] This research led to the important discovery that **feelings— specifically, how people feel *at* work and how they feel *about* their work—determine employee well-being.**

The Key Drivers of Well-Being

Employee well-being encompasses far more than just job satisfaction and workplace happiness. It includes a thorough consideration of an individual's physical, emotional, and mental health, along with their work-life balance. Genuine well-being is also shaped by having a sense of purpose in one's role, the freedom to determine when and where to work, and opportunities for ongoing personal and professional development.

Essentially, De Neve determined that it really boils down to the culture of one's organization and the impact and influence of its leaders. *Do employees feel they work in an environment where they can thrive both professionally and personally?*

The Most Surprising Driver of Well-Being of All

De Neve's most unexpected and profound conclusion is that the greatest driver of employee well-being is *belonging.*

A sense of belonging comes when workers feel their organizations, managers, and colleagues care about them personally. It comes when their workplace consistently meets their social needs for friendship, connection, and appreciation. It comes when they feel there is diversity, inclusion, and trust in their workplace, and when people work collaboratively, as a team.

It's little surprise that De Neve also discovered that very few workplace leaders today grasp the importance of fostering belonging within their teams. Just 6 percent of leaders who were surveyed rated "belonging" as a primary driver of employee happiness at work, and only a third (34 percent) ranked it among the top five drivers.[15]

How Well-Being Affects Productivity

Over a six-month period, De Neve conducted a separate study at a British Telecom call center where he asked employees to describe how happy they felt at the end of every work week by choosing one of five emojis representing their overall level of contentment: a very happy face, a happy face, a neutral face, a sad face, or a very unhappy face (see figure 1).[16]

De Neve then compared this simple, straightforward, and easy-to-solicit feedback to employee performance data the organization regularly tracked, such as the number of calls people handled, customer satisfaction per call, time spent per call, and daily sales. He found that productivity was directly related to how workers felt in any given week—meaning that the higher the sense of well-being workers reported, the better the call center's overall performance was.

As an economist, De Neve later proved that traditional financial impacts like return on assets, profits, and a firm's value also have a direct and positive correlation to employee well-being.[17] And he isn't alone in discovering that investing in worker well-being can improve retention and productivity:

▧ Research by Gallup found that companies with high levels of employee well-being have a 27 percent higher profitability rate compared to those with low levels.[18]

FIGURE 1. Smiley face rating scale used for self-reporting of employee well-being

- Researchers at the London School of Economics, in collaboration with Gallup, conducted a study covering 1.8 million employees across 73 countries. They concluded that higher employee well-being correlates directly with increased productivity, customer satisfaction, and profitability.[19]

- Case studies in the Global Council for Happiness and Wellbeing's 2019 policy report showed that organizations with robust well-being programs experience improved financial outcomes and lower employee turnover.[20]

Unfortunately, while well-being programs are common in organizations these days, evidence of their success has been hard to find.[21] For instance, De Neve's colleague, fellow Oxford researcher William Fleming, analyzed survey responses from 46,336 workers and found that company-sponsored mental health resources ("wellness benefits") had no significant impact on worker well-being.[22] More specifically, he found that employees who took advantage of available resources such as wellness programs, sleep apps, and resilience and stress management classes were no better off than their colleagues who never used them.[23]

This Book Will Teach You How to Elevate Your Team's Well-Being

What all of this means for us as leaders is that the stakes have now been raised. All of the human beings who work for us have profound new (and permanent) expectations of work, and we must meet those expectations if we are to retain them and inspire the best from them.

According to a February 2024 survey from American automaker Ford, 52 percent of polled employees worldwide said they would take a 20 percent pay cut to achieve a lifestyle that prioritized their well-being and quality of life.[24] Other recent studies have found similar results, highlighting a growing trend of employees prioritizing work-life balance over higher pay. The legacy of COVID has undoubtedly influenced this trend, which signals that work is no longer the sole focus of many people's lives. This represents a major shift away from the Industrial Age view that work must always take precedence.

To restate the obvious, company leaders cannot sustainably improve employee well-being simply by measuring it (remember, we tried this unsuccessfully with employee engagement)—and no generic "well-being" or "wellness" program will provide the solution either.

As a point of clarity and important reiteration, I define "employee well-being" specifically within a workplace context. Here, we focus on how to create a positive and nurturing workplace culture—one that addresses what employees everywhere today seek from their experience at work: a caring and appreciative boss, a sense of belonging, a collaborative environment, manageable workloads, emotional and mental health, professional development, work-life balance, and fair treatment.

In our framework, we will address employee well-being in terms of ensuring that people feel valued, respected, deeply connected to their colleagues, and empowered in their roles, not in terms of personal health practices such as diet, exercise, or spirituality.

This is crucial because when people perceive their personal well-being as high at work, their individual productivity tends to be high as well. The bottom line is that how people assess their personal well-being is one of the greatest drivers of their dedication and performance.

In their book *It's the Manager: Moving from Boss to Coach*, former Gallup CEO Jim Clifton and Chief Scientist Jim Harter conclude that managers account for 70 percent of the variance in overall team performance.[25] From this, we can impute that **the practices and behavior of a team manager largely determine the degree of well-being any team experiences**.

As few C-suites have directly tasked workplace managers with supporting employee well-being (traditionally, their job has only been to drive performance and ensure goals are met), managers will now need a concise guide—a road map—to use in helping their people thrive, flourish, *and* perform optimally.

And that's exactly what this book is.

This book is written for managers at all levels, in organizations of all sizes and industries. It will show you how you can personally, positively, and directly affect the well-being of the people you lead, and build an uncommonly successful team through your efforts.

Throughout my decades as a senior leader, and for the past fifteen years as an author and consultant, I have been living and breathing workplace leadership—most notably by digesting a preponderance of research that proves there are far more enlightened and informed ways of motivating employee performance than we've historically believed.

In 2011, I wrote the first edition of a book that eleven American universities have since used in their classrooms. In *Lead from the Heart: Transformational Leadership for the 21st Century*, I argued that traditional workplace management practices were failing workers and organizations, and that emerging science had proven that human beings actually perform best when they feel valued, esteemed, cared for, developed, appreciated—even nurtured (we've since learned that all of these are key drivers of well-being).

And while I already had truly compelling data and evidence to validate my thesis, leaders nevertheless met me with instinctive skepticism.

The idea of caring or leading with any amount of heart sounded incredibly soft and weak to a lot of people in business. While disappointing to me, this response nevertheless made sense in light of traditional leadership theory, which had always advocated for squeezing workers, not nurturing them in any consequential way.

Slowly but surely, I committed myself to winning over workplace managers by presenting on stages and in articles as much evidence as I could find that demonstrated that our traditional ways of leading people were entirely misaligned to human nature.

I read scores of books in myriad genres, including over 150 written by the world-class academics, researchers, and CEOs I went on to interview on my *Lead from the Heart* podcast.[26] And, in 2022, I wrote a second edition of my book, imbued with the most up-to-date knowledge I'd acquired.

Now, in this new book, my goal is to make you the beneficiary of all my experience in helping managers to nurture employee well-being while simultaneously achieving high performance—and to make the conclusions I've reached actionable with the least required investment of *your* time.

I've presented my ideas in brief chapters, like a primer. While they indeed have a through-line, each chapter stands on its own. At the end of many of them, I'll challenge you to put the information you just learned to immediate use.

In the end, we retain from our studies
only that which we practically apply.

—JOHANN WOLFGANG VON GOETHE[27]

1

Connecting the Dots

The whole is greater than the sum of its parts.

—ARISTOTLE[1]

The late Dr. Spencer Johnson wrote two of the bestselling business books of all time, *Who Moved My Cheese?* and *The One Minute Manager* (cowritten with Ken Blanchard). Both of them are uncommonly short, just a hundred pages or so.

Dr. Johnson once told me that the length of his books was no accident; he had been highly influenced by Charles Caleb Colton, who said, "The most effective writer imparts the most knowledge while taking the least amount of time from the reader."

Although this book exceeds a hundred pages, it has been written with the same inspiration that guided Dr. Johnson: the chapters are brief and compact. Before you read them, I want to quickly explain how they're all related and how each contributes to the whole.

In 2004, Nobel Laureate Daniel Kahneman and a group of other highly esteemed researchers published a study titled "A Survey Method for Characterizing Daily Life Experience: The Day Reconstruction

Method."[2] Instead of relying on traditional survey methods, which the team deemed to be imperfect and often influenced by memory bias, they invented an entirely new research approach by asking study participants (workers) to reconstruct their previous day's activities and experiences for the purpose of understanding the emotional quality of their daily lives and the factors that contribute to well-being.

The results of their analysis of the survey responses make it clear that most managers are far from effectively supporting the well-being of their people. Notably, Kahneman's team found that:

- Of all the people workers interact with, bosses are their least favorite, coming in after coworkers and clients/customers.

- Work ranks among the least enjoyable aspects of workers' daily lives, second only to commuting to and from the office.

Based on these findings, it would seem reasonable to conclude not only that managers' practices, attitudes, and behavior play a crucial role in shaping employees' overall well-being, but that there are a lot of managers around the world who have a suboptimal impact on their people.

You may be thinking, "I'm glad I'm not one of them." Whether that's actually true or not, during the time you spend reading this book, I would ask you to suspend any disbelief that *you* might also be the kind of manager employees dread.

Here's why.

I don't believe most workplace managers come to work every day with the intention of being a harmful influence on the people they lead. Rather, I'm convinced that many, many managers are simply unaware of the behaviors and practices that support well-being, and therefore unwittingly neglect to do the very things that would help their employees thrive.

The following chapters aim to teach you the specific things science now proves directly contribute to human flourishing. Approaching them with a growth mindset—open-mindedness—will ensure you gain the most from your investment of time in reading them.

Here's a quick overview of what's coming:

Chapter 2: Know Thyself

Becoming the kind of leader people everywhere now hunger to work for demands of us both an inner and an outer transformation. We first must do the deep work of truly discovering who we are—what makes us tick. We begin here because deep self-awareness enables leaders to lead authentically and build trust and credibility with their teams. We can't effectively lead others without first knowing ourselves.

Chapter 3: Drop a Pin

Investing time in defining clear personal values helps leaders make consistent and fair decisions. When leaders' actions are aligned with their values, they also create a work environment that reflects those values— and this positive environment fosters employee trust, motivation, and well-being.

Chapter 4: Emotions Power the Workplace

Surprising research proves *emotions play an outsized role in influencing employee behavior and performance* (we humans are not as rational as we believe). By understanding and addressing the emotional needs of their employees, leaders can significantly enhance their commitment, loyalty, and productivity—and help them thrive.

Chapter 5: Embrace Our Shared Humanity

We must embrace the idea that human beings are complicated; even messy at times. Expecting people to be on their best behavior all the time simply ignores reality (that goes for us human leaders, too). When we know people can be messy, we're more inclined to be patient, tolerant, and open to diverse perspectives—all of which helps make our people feel safe.

Chapter 6: Curate Connection and Belonging

As you read in the Introduction, a sense of belonging in the workplace is the single greatest driver of employee well-being. It fulfills the essential human need to feel known, valued, and appreciated by others. Employees who have close relationships at work are more likely to be part of high-performing teams and experience greater job satisfaction. Post-pandemic shifts toward remote and hybrid work have weakened these ties, making it crucial for leaders to foster connection and belonging within our teams.

Chapter 7: Be a Positive Force

Research shows that experiencing a high ratio of positive to negative interactions and emotions is crucial for the well-being of relationships—especially between employees and managers. Once you realize that, this chapter's title is your call to action.

Chapter 8: Turn Over Every Stone

Managers of yesteryear thought they needed to have all the answers and to always be in control. Today, when the world we live in is so frequently unpredictable and ambiguous, this is a mismatched approach to leadership. This understanding naturally influences us to become more curious, more open to learning and to giving other people a voice—and to routinely challenge our own assumptions. It's a shift in approach that supports employee well-being by fostering an environment of collaboration, experimentation, and open communication.

Chapter 9: Step into the Fog

When leaders accept that life is often ambiguous and unpredictable, we embrace a calm and optimistic approach to challenges. Instead of being rigidly tied to a single plan, our teams can dynamically adjust to changing conditions, reducing stress. This supportive atmosphere encourages innovation and resilience, contributing to a positive and thriving workplace.

Chapter 10: Loosen Your Grip

An ongoing fifty-year UK study revealed that employees who have the most control over their work schedules experience longer lifespans and fewer heart attacks and strokes. Giving employees more autonomy and flexibility directly elevates their well-being.

Chapter 11: We Instead of Me

Research shows that teams that are highly cooperative and collaborative perform better and are healthier. Leaders who emphasize mutual support unlock their teams' full potential—a great contrast with internal competition, which undermines teamwork and morale.

Chapter 12: Growth Creates Happiness

Humans are happiest when we are growing. When leaders identify their people's talents and potential and actively help develop them, we create a culture of growth that yields optimal performance.

Chapter 13: Care About—Even Love—Your People

When Dean Smith retired after thirty-six seasons as head coach of the men's basketball team at the University of North Carolina at Chapel Hill, he was the most successful collegiate basketball coach in US history. His success was rooted in genuinely caring for his players—a philosophy that now must extend to workplace management. Like Smith, effective managers build caring relationships, fostering an environment where employees thrive and excel.

By embracing all of the strategies you're about to read about, you'll cultivate a high-performing team that's grounded in well-being. Each chapter brims with actionable insights that can transform your leadership practice and help you create a workplace environment so compelling that people will be drawn to be part of the culture you've built.

Okay, let's dive in!

2

Know Thyself

Knowing yourself is the beginning of all wisdom.

—ARISTOTLE[1]

Managers who invest in self-awareness lay the groundwork for a supportive and thriving workplace environment. So, this book begins with a direct challenge for you to devote time and energy to your own self-discovery, and to emerge from it deeply knowing thyself. When managers fail to do this important work, they risk miscommunicating, lacking empathy, and making decisions inconsistently—all of which directly undermine employee trust and well-being. Bottom line: None of us can successfully lead other people until we know ourselves.

Our ability to connect with and relate to all of the people we manage depends upon how accurately we know our own strengths, limitations, formative life experiences, motivations, fears, emotional triggers, and biases—not to mention how other people perceive us.

As I've mentioned, leaders who know themselves in this way are far more likely to empathize with others. When we know our own struggles, we can better relate to the challenges faced by our people. And by comprehending all of the forces that influence our own thinking, we are able to make more informed, consistent, and therefore successful decisions and choices.

Suffice it to say, it's a rare workplace manager who has gained this high degree of self-discernment—and not just because it demands intentional focus and a lifelong commitment to self-discovery. The higher hurdle is that most leaders don't believe they need to do this work at all. Research shows that 95 percent of people *believe* they are self-aware, while just 10–15 percent (at best) truly *are*.[2]

When we as leaders don't put in the work to know ourselves, we miss out on massive growth opportunities that can elevate our future effectiveness. We remain stagnant, repeating the same ineffective patterns and practices over and over. The upside to gaining true self-awareness is huge—the return on investment is just too high to pass up!

Truth be told, I was once in the camp of leaders who believed they already fully understood themselves and had little more to learn. Then, a team exercise set me straight.

After I thought I'd been excelling in a senior management role for over a year at one of America's largest financial institutions, I attended a meeting with my boss and a dozen of my peers. Our human resources business partner was there to facilitate the discussion, and after briefly explaining what we were about to do, she handed each of us a stack of blank index cards and asked us to write down two things we admired greatly about every person in the room. This meant that each of us would go on to hear twenty-six pieces of meaningful praise.

When the facilitator got to me and read all of the glowing things everyone had anonymously written about me, I felt triumphant. So much of what my colleagues said confirmed that I was doing a great job as a leader and that my impact was being widely seen and felt.

Once the facilitator had finished reading and discussing everyone's positive leadership traits, she asked us to write down one piece of constructive feedback for each person: *What's one thing you wish this person knew was hindering their leadership effectiveness?*

This time, when she got to me and read out what everyone had written, I visibly winced. To a person, my peers wanted me to know that I could be sarcastic at times, and that my sarcasm was hurtful and weakened others' respect for me.

Hearing that I was perceived this way completely blindsided me—and the revelation was made even more painful by the fact that my overriding motivation had always been to leave people feeling good whenever they interacted with me.

Even before our team meeting was over, I started asking myself what could have influenced me to be so sarcastic at work. And I soon had a powerful epiphany. Throughout my childhood, my father was routinely critical and demeaning, and he used sarcasm widely to disparage me and others. Unconsciously, I had clearly adopted his toxic behavior, and it was only because of the candor of the people closest to me that it got called out. Had I not received this critique, I never would have taken steps to eliminate the behavior. And by never having made the improvement, I likely would have derailed my leadership career.

If you make the commitment to fully "know thyself" (and I urge you to), the best place to start is to write down a list of your leadership strengths and weaknesses as you see them,[3] and then solicit feedback from trusted friends, family members, and colleagues for comparison. *Do other people see you as you see you?*

One reason many people don't take this initial step is because hearing constructive criticism (learning we are limited) can be painful—so, we'd just as soon avoid it.

But when we realize that there is no such thing as a self-actualized leader, and that every workplace manager is a work in progress, it becomes much easier to accept that we too might have some areas of improvement requiring our attention.

As I learned in the exercise with my peers, asking people to identify two of your greatest strengths opens the door to them feeling comfortable pointing out just one weakness. The key is to solicit responses from several of the people who know you best.

As you might expect, some people find it really uncomfortable to deliver truly critical feedback—especially to someone they like and whose feelings they don't want to hurt. So, it's important to give anyone you ask for input full permission to be candid, and you must persist until you get at least one answer to this question: *What's one thing you believe significantly limits me as a leader?*

Once you have clearly identified your strengths and weaknesses, it's time for the even more important work of reflecting upon what Harvard Business School professor Bill George calls the "crucible moments" of your life.[4]

What are the are the most significant trials or painful events that you've endured in your life? Parents getting divorced, deaths in the family, financial setbacks, dealing with addiction—destabilizing experiences like these can take a lasting toll. The goal is to bring them into your awareness and to ask yourself how they may be continuing to influence you in your interactions with people today. Many people are stunned to discover the extent to which they actually do.

It's also important for you to retrace how you navigated those challenges. Consider how you maneuvered through your past fears, disappointments, and failures. Reflecting on your most difficult setbacks and how you dealt with them will ensure you not only learn from them but can go on to apply all of your hard-earned wisdom to the future stressful events you'll inevitably face. Life's toughest and most painful experiences can carry great lessons once we bring those insights into the light.

It's undeniable that human behavior is often unconsciously influenced by childhood experiences (this is true for you, and also for everyone you manage). If someone grew up with a perfectionistic or harshly critical parent, for example, they might be triggered by a boss who rarely appreciates them, not realizing that their negative emotional response is more directly tied to their past experiences than to their present one. Simply being aware that emotionally charged events in our upbringing can resurface in our adult lives can help us avoid unnecessary conflicts with people. When we ask ourselves, "Why is this person getting under my skin?" we may quickly realize the problem is more about us than it is about them.

When we devote intentional time and effort to excavating our past, we not only come to truly understand our motivations and triggers, we also become more self-confident. And we don't just become more secure in our own skin; we gain invaluable insight into the motivations and behavior of others. The payoff for knowing thyself is leadership mastery.

The Work of a Lifetime

As mentioned earlier, cultivating extensive self-awareness is a lifelong journey, not just a one-and-done exercise. So always remember, your leadership effectiveness will grow over time as your self-awareness expands.

The most enlightened leaders I've known seemed to intuitively understand this and made a regular practice of avoiding the self-deception that every action they would take, and every decision they would make, would land as planned. Instead, they intentionally built a routine of reflecting upon their choices and considering how they impacted others. When outcomes proved suboptimal, they would take the learning with them and adjust their approach in the future. And as one more example of how a truly self-aware leader operates in the world, they avoided reflexively blaming others for problems that occurred before evaluating their own role in creating them.

Final Thoughts

Once you have asked your friends, peers, employees—even boss—to share their observations about your leadership strengths and current limitations, consider sharing all the feedback you received with them. Tell them all the things you learned, and what you are now most committed to improving. Having the courage to do this will not only demonstrate that you took everyone's insights seriously, it will also model the behavior you want from them. Most importantly, it will ensure you have some accountability for doing better. And, believe me, they'll all be watching.

There is one more critical step in your process of knowing yourself; we'll explore this next.

3

Drop a Pin

I have one important piece of advice I want to share—
so important that it's the only piece of advice I'm going to
share today. And that is this: Whatever you do, lead with your
values. By leading with your values, what I mean is that you should
make decisions, big and small, each and every day, based on a deep
understanding of who you are and what you believe.

—TIM COOK, Apple CEO
addressing the graduating class of
Gallaudet University in 2022[1]

Have you ever wondered what uniquely characterizes people who excel in high-stress situations—the astronauts, surgeons, star athletes, even leaders who are able to stare down fear and execute the best possible actions in "make or break," or even life or death, moments?

When Dr. Eric Potterat, high-performance psychologist and coauthor of *Learned Excellence: Mental Disciplines for Leading and Winning from the World's Top Performers*,[2] joined me on my podcast in 2024, I asked him to answer that question, knowing he was uniquely qualified to do so. Potterat helped create the mental toughness curriculum used during US Navy Seals training, and he has worked with nearly 25,000 elite performers across various fields, including the World Series–winning Los Angeles Dodgers and the US women's national soccer team.

"We tend to believe that all superior performers are born winners," Potterat told me, "but we all know plenty of talented people who never achieve elite status. Talent alone is never enough."[3]

What actually proves to differentiate superstar performers, Potterat said, is a mastery of four learned behaviors. Importantly, he stressed that this same self-mastery is available to all of us, as long as we dedicate ourselves to integrating these same four behaviors into our daily lives. According to Potterat, high performers:

- **Are highly resilient.** They recover quickly from setbacks and emerge stronger. They embrace the idea that success and failure are deeply intertwined and view obstacles as opportunities for growth and learning, not as insurmountable barriers.

- **Commit to making incremental improvements.** Tied to a growth mindset, they dedicate themselves to making *small, continuous changes* to elevate their effectiveness, efficiency, and overall performance. They habitually challenge themselves to refine their skills and grow over time.

- **Keep their minds focused on the only three things they can directly control: their *attitude*, their *effort*, and their *actions*.** They've learned to tune out all external voices and inputs that can distract them or otherwise undermine their performance. By concentrating only on what they can influence or change, they become proactive rather than reactive.

- **Have highly refined value systems and have developed a personal "credo."** This final attribute may surprise you, and it is the real focus of this chapter. Taking a desire to "know thyself" to a distinctly higher level, high performers define their personal values with the greatest precision and then use that as a touchstone to guide their future behavior and choices. They review their credo daily, and have built up the discipline to filter *every important decision they make* through it.

Credo comes from the Latin word meaning "I believe." The serious work in creating a personal credo comes in asking ourselves who we really want to be as a person, and what values we most believe in—and then distilling all of that into a ten-word list.

When it comes to important issues, values allow you to have radical flexibility. Once you've defined your values clearly, you don't have to weigh the pros and cons every time you are faced with a decision. It's already been made for you.

—ROLF DOBELLI,
author of *The Art of the Good Life*[4]

How is this relevant in leadership? Often, in very stressful and challenging situations, managers must quickly make important and consequential decisions. When they have invested time and thought into defining exactly what they personally stand for, they are prepared to ask themselves, "Is this decision I'm about to make aligned to who I am at my core?" This serves as a reminder in the moment not to conform, but to stick to their credo and do what they believe is best.

In contrast, Potterat says non-elite performers often lack a reliable compass to guide their lives, and therefore routinely fall prey to the influence of their peers and other social pressures: "They act not of their own rock-solid values, but of what others around them think of them."[5]

There's another reason personal credos hold so much beneficial power: most people build them with wildly positive and humane words, such as trustworthy, inclusive, respectful, curious, fair, appreciative, and caring. These words are inherently aligned with the goal of sustaining employee well-being.

*Who's not going to like someone who routinely displays
trust, advocacy, and equanimity? When someone is
values-driven, people can see it a mile away. It has a
profound influence on people. It's transformational.*

—ERIC POTTERAT[6]

It's safe to assume that many workplace managers today have not invested the time and focus required to produce their own personal credos. But let's not use this assumption as an excuse to avoid preparing one ourselves. Defining one's personal values has become essential in leadership because it yields clarity, guides ethical and consistent decision-making, and builds trust. Managers who put in the time and effort to articulate and live by their values can lead their teams with integrity and purpose, ultimately supporting the well-being and success of their people.

If you were wondering, the phrase "drop a pin" means to mark a particular location on a map for easy access. When defining personal values, I employ this metaphor to describe pinpointing and clearly marking what's most important to you personally. Just as you would drop a pin on a map to highlight a significant spot, you drop a pin on each of your core values so that they can direct your decisions and actions. Your values, in essence, act as your personal GPS, guiding you along your leadership path.

Final Thoughts

When you begin working on creating your own credo, keep in mind that its underlying purpose is to help you know yourself deeply. You needn't (and really shouldn't) complete it quickly, and the ten words you ultimately choose should best describe the most authentic you. These words should inspire you, and they should succinctly describe not only the leader you aspire to be, but also the leader you plan to hold yourself accountable to being.

A well-defined credo will shape your behavior, decisions, and overall way of life. It will directly influence how you interact with the world around you. A personal credo serves as your true north, but it's not set in stone. In fact, I recommend revising it over time as life experiences continue to clarify what matters most to you.

Take a few minutes now to start developing your own credo. Jot down a list of values you already know in your heart that you want to embody. Then, commit to refining your list over the coming days and weeks, and boil it down to the words that will rouse you to be the person and leader that, deep down, you really want to be.

4

Emotions Power
the Workplace

*Most men seem to live according
to sense rather than reason.*

—SIR THOMAS AQUINAS[1]

Nearly 2,500 years ago, the Greek philosopher Plato posited that emotions and rationality worked harmoniously together in influencing human behavior and decision-making. Soon after, however, as Leonard Mlodinow describes in his book *Emotional: How Feelings Shape Our Thinking*, his views were widely spurned: "After Plato, those two aspects of our life came to be seen as working in opposition to each other. Reason was viewed as superior and even holy. Emotions were to be avoided or contained."[2]

In the 17th century, French philosopher René Descartes famously declared, "I think, therefore I am"—an authoritative assertion that human beings are fundamentally rational.[3] Descartes was so convincing at the time that his decree became gospel—and, ever since, we've commonly accepted that feelings and emotions are unreliable sources of information, internal interferences that only get in the way of sound judgment.

Workplace leadership, of course, has long taken its cue from Descartes by purposely marginalizing feelings and emotions—including intuition—in decision-making. Businesses intentionally hire the "brainiest" people for management roles, and have traditionally sought to motivate employee performance through logic and reasoning.

But now, over two millennia after Plato's time and nearly four centuries after Descartes', scientists have discovered that human beings aren't purely rational after all. In fact, feelings and emotions have been shown to play an oversized role in influencing our actions and choices. The rather important leadership takeaway here is that how managers make us *feel*, and not what they make us *think*, drives employee commitment, loyalty, productivity, and well-being.

In his book *Descartes' Error: Emotion, Reason, and the Human Brain*,[4] Salk Institute neuroscientist Antonio Damasio was first to prove that feelings are a powerful force on reason and unconsciously steer thought. He asserted that emotions largely determine our behavior and influence what we devote our attention to at any given moment.

Some readers may bristle at Damasio's conclusion, preferring to believe that they are the exception to the rule and remain wholly rational in everything they do. But as Damasio explains, even though we may feel certain we're being entirely rational at all times, feelings and emotions routinely influence our behavior outside of our conscious awareness.

> *Emotion shapes virtually every thought we have.*
> *It contributes, moment to moment,*
> *to all our judgments and decisions.*
>
> —LEONARD MLODINOW[5]

Since Damasio's groundbreaking work, several more academics have firmly confirmed his research. In fact, according to Zoe Chance, Yale University School of Management professor and author of *Influence*

Is Your Superpower, some researchers have estimated that feelings and emotions may be *solely* responsible for up to 95 percent of our decisions and behavior.[6]

This phenomenon is increasingly being recognized in the workplace. As Marc Brackett, Yale University research psychologist and author of *Permission to Feel: Unlocking the Power of Emotions to Help Our Kids, Ourselves, and Our Society Thrive*, explains, leaders now are challenged to understand the role emotions play in influencing employee performance. According to Brackett, "Everything that happens at work is at heart an emotional moment. 'I deserve a promotion,' for example, means 'I'm worth more than you realize.'"[7]

Late Wharton Business School management professor Sigal Barsade was a pioneer in what organizational psychologists call "the affective revolution"—the study of how emotions, not just behavior and decision-making, shape workplace culture, and, in turn, how they affect an organization's performance. As she observed, "For a long time, emotions were viewed as noise, a nuisance, something to be ignored. But one thing we now know after more than a quarter-century of research is that emotions are not noise—rather, they are data. They reveal not just how people feel, but also what they think and how they will behave."[8]

> *Because emotions play such a role in driving employee performance, if you ignore them, you're really managing with one hand tied behind your back. Emotions influence how long people stay, how well they perform, and how well they interact with others.*
>
> —SIGAL BARSADE[9]

Feelings Drive Behavior

As we've just seen, employee behavior (ours included) is biologically connected to feelings. So, if we want to get people to commit, to innovate, to connect with others, and to contribute to their highest potential, we must actively and intentionally affect their emotional side, which directly informs their behavior.

In her book *Energy Rising: The Neuroscience of Leading with Emotional Power*, neuropsychologist Julia DiGangi says that human emotions influence people to experience feelings of either "pain" or "power."[10]

Stress, anxiety, fear, anger, worry, frustration, and disappointment all produce emotional pain (harmful to well-being).

Any sensation that makes us feel worthy, confident, strong, esteemed, significant, or important elevates our feeling of power (supportive to well-being).

This is consistent with what Brackett found when he asked people for three words to describe what they most wanted to feel at work. Predictably, "happy" was the number one choice, followed by related words such as excited, joyful, appreciated, supported, fulfilled, respected, inspired, and accomplished.[11]

These kinds of feelings prove to inspire optimal human performance—*and* optimal well-being. We can be certain that workers have long yearned to experience these "power"-inspiring emotions at work. It's only now that we're discovering how essential it is that they do.

To make one's employees consistently *feel* powerful, leaders must truly care about them personally. We mustn't conflate caring for people with lowering performance expectations or no longer holding employees accountable for results. Caring about one's team doesn't conflict with setting a high bar. It simply means that while pursuing our goals, we concurrently show employees interest, kindness, honesty, fairness, and appreciation.

Give your people opportunities to grow and develop. Find ways to encourage them. Coach them, and help build their confidence. Remind them of how much their work matters and how it makes a difference. Never forget that any positive emotion that influences human beings to feel powerful in turn makes them more enthusiastic, invested, and content in their work.

Final Thoughts

If you pause for a moment to think about who was the most influential— or "best"—manager you've ever had in your career, it's almost certain that you will describe that person as someone who cared about you personally, and who found myriad ways to make you feel safe, valued, and powerful.

> *I've learned that people will forget what you said,*
> *people will forget what you did, but people*
> *will never forget how you made them feel.*
>
> —MAYA ANGELOU, poet and Nobel Laureate[12]

Angelou's wisdom—essential knowledge for workplace managers— is that people respond to and remember how we interact with them, far beyond our factual exchanges. People who work for you and with you will largely judge your influence, and your leadership effectiveness, by how you make them feel. And how people feel at work largely determines how they'll assess their own overall well-being.

5

Embrace Our Shared Humanity

Every human will frustrate, anger, annoy,
madden and disappoint us, and we will
(without any malice) do the same to them.

—ALAIN DE BOTTON[1]

While most of us will probably learn our most valuable leadership lessons through our own direct experience in managing people, there's one crucial insight that managers should learn early, even before assuming a leadership role: *Dealing with human beings can be truly exhausting at times. We are all inherently messy, complex, and imperfect.*

Of course, we all know people come to the workplace with their own unique personalities and motivations. Nevertheless, one of the greatest sources of frustration and stress in management comes from situations where other people behave in ways we don't see as appropriate or don't quite understand.[2]

For starters, plenty of research proves that people tend to be more accepting of people like themselves. We've all heard the adage that "opposites attract," but the truth is, we human beings are hardwired to gravitate toward similar and like-minded people.[3]

So, our first piece of guidance is to realize that one reason we may find ourselves in difficulty with other people is simply because they approach certain aspects of life very differently than we do. And we unwittingly allow their methods to irritate us.

Our second piece of guidance is to realize that any expectation that the people around us should think and behave just like we do is entirely unrealistic.

Most of our colleagues and employees come to the workplace with past experiences and cultural upbringings very unlike our own. Their educational backgrounds, knowledge, talents, and skills naturally vary greatly. Some are introverted, others extroverted. They're at myriad stages of life and have wildly divergent aspirations at work. Even when not directly disclosed, they often possess highly diverse spiritual and philosophical views.

All of this individual diversity should remind us that while people do indeed share many commonalities, more often than not, our differences are strengths that we should purposefully embrace. In other words, we're wise to accept each other as we are. Besides, trying to change people simply never works. As legendary music producer Rick Rubin sagely observes, "We're all different and we're all imperfect and the imperfections are what makes each of us and our work interesting."[4]

The messiness of people also comes into play when employees experience personal challenges, such as a divorce, a child who's struggling at school, the need to care for an elderly parent, or an illness of their own. There once was a day when workers were told to "leave your troubles at the door," a clear and inhumane effort by managers to prevent having to deal with human messiness during work hours.

Today, experienced leaders intuitively understand that ignoring an employee's suffering, or expecting them to suppress it while at work, will only further compromise their well-being, as well as that of the team. On the other hand, showing interest, empathy, and compassion—and perhaps even finding ways to make scheduling or workload accommodations—demonstrates to people, in crucial moments, that they truly matter to you.

What's more, it's always been my experience that when employees are made to feel that they are valued as human beings, they will instinctively reciprocate by taking steps to minimize, as much as possible, any impact the personal challenges they are facing might have on the responsibilities they have at work.

Also, remember that people commonly conduct themselves in unexpected and unpredictable ways because human behavior is naturally less rational and more emotional. As psychotherapist and *Financial Times* columnist Naomi Shragai observes in her book *The Man Who Mistook His Job for His Life*, this reality often presents the biggest challenge a manager will ever face. There is, she says, "[a] lingering false notion that work is a predominantly rational and objective world with specific goals, largely free of emotions." Yet, "Alongside our skills, dedication and ambition, we bring to the office our 'inner lives'—our sensitivities, misperceptions, fears and insecurities—the strong emotions that at times hijack us."[5]

As Shragai notes, employees' behavior at work is often an unconscious reenactment of conflicts and relationships they've experienced elsewhere in their lives, and not a response to an immediate work situation. With this insight in mind, our goal as managers must be to cultivate the emotional maturity and patience required to understand and support employees exhibiting challenging or emotionally charged behavior. Rather than judge people's idiosyncrasies, we should more eagerly accept and adapt to them. We surely have many of our own.

Unless, of course, someone's behavior is unacceptably or chronically disruptive and inappropriate (in which case it must be directly addressed), a leader's most informed response is to intentionally display some tolerance and understanding. Accept that people will go off the rails occasionally, and that giving them a little space and grace is exactly what they'll need in order to get themselves back on track.

It's also human nature to assume that in virtually all disputes we find ourselves involved in, the other person is surely to blame. However, insightful leaders understand that they likely play a part in most disagreements, noting that they're rarely ever solely someone else's fault.

So, whenever you're dealing with the messiness of people, remember the words of self-compassion guru Dr. Kristin Neff: "When faced with our human imperfection, we can either respond with kindness and care, or with judgment and criticism."[6]

Never forget, we're all works in progress!

Final Thoughts

Whenever a conflict arises, take a few deep breaths before choosing your response. Try to shift your perspective to see a bigger picture of what is happening.

With practice, you'll gain a more instinctive understanding of which differences with people can be solved through tolerance and restraint, and which will require intervention and redirection.

Another highly useful piece of advice is to refrain from personalizing someone else's behavior. Taking things personally is a common—and natural—human tendency, but what other people do or say isn't always about you. Even when situations seem personal, such as when someone insults us, is curt to us, or is otherwise unkind, their actions are rarely entirely about us and almost always say a lot more about them. These moments provide valuable clues into other people's issues, if we can remain still and pay attention.

You'll avoid a lot of future pain and stress and gain a lot of insight by remembering this.

6

Curate Connection
and Belonging

*We are psychologically, emotionally, cognitively, and
spiritually hardwired for connection, love, and belonging. . . .
It is why we are here, and it is what gives purpose
and meaning to our lives.*

—BRENÉ BROWN[1]

In light of the myriad responsibilities workplace managers already
have piled high on their plates, asking them to take responsibility for
ensuring the people on their teams feel deeply connected to one another
might seem like an unreasonable, and even nonessential, task.

Not so.

A 2022 Gartner survey of nearly 3,500 employees found that when
organizations intentionally help employees build relationships, their
people are five times more likely to be on a high-performing team and
twelve times as likely to feel personally connected to their colleagues.[2]

No one is an island, as the saying goes. We are made to support one
another—and employee health and happiness are directly tied to having

close relational bonds. This is because feeling known, valued, and appreciated by others is a foundational human need.

It wasn't that long ago that we all worked closely together in offices every day, making it much easier to forge tight relationships. But after the COVID-19 pandemic physically separated many of us for over a year, hybrid work schedules permanently reduced the number of day-to-day, face-to-face interactions we had with one another. Even when working together on designated office days, it's become normalized for many of us to stay in our offices, cubes, and cubbies, and to take meetings online rather than in person with colleagues who are sitting nearby.

The result is that today we have much weaker ties with our coworkers, invisibly undermining individual well-being and team cohesiveness at the same time.

Thirty years ago, according to Gallup research, nearly half of all Americans had a best friend at work.[3] But by 2024, that number had fallen to just one in five.[4] This sharp decline is even more notable because Gallup research has long shown that employees are far more dedicated, content in their jobs, and likely to remain working at an organization when they have close friendships at work.[5]

In March 2020, the onset of the pandemic confined millions of workers around the world to their homes. While inherently disruptive in so many ways, the work-from-home experience eliminated daily commutes to and from our workplaces—a luxury many of us were reluctant to give up once offices reopened a year or more later.

When companies finally began putting pressure on employees to return to the office on a much more frequent basis, many argued that a key reason they wanted everyone back was because working together would help restore the team "connection" that had been eroded during the lockdown. But at that time, many workers weren't buying it, stating they felt they already had sufficient interactions with friends and family members during non-work hours to sustain them. Work friendships, in other words, had lost their importance.

Confirming this sentiment, in March 2022, software company Capterra asked a thousand American workers to rank the relative importance of fourteen job satisfaction factors, such as "job security," "learning opportunities," "recognition," and "compensation." Respondents ranked "relationships with coworkers" the least important of all the factors. Only 11 percent of workers listed it in their top three.[6]

Just one year later, however, many people began to have a change of heart, realizing they were hungering for more in-person interactions with their work colleagues.

When customer research management firm HubSpot surveyed over 5,000 remote, in-office, and hybrid workers as part of their 2023 Hybrid Work Report, they found employees were now "craving connection and community more than ever."[7] Stunningly, when given the choice, 52 percent of the survey respondents said they'd prioritize "fostering great relationships with their colleagues" over receiving a 10 percent salary increase. The team concluded, "Our research is clear—the new frontier in the future of work is creating ways for employees to connect with their company's culture, purpose, and each other."

Lost Connection

Even before the COVID-19 pandemic, from 2003 to 2019, the average amount of free time Americans reported spending alone had increased by 5 percentage points—and at the height of the pandemic in 2020, people were spending more than half of their free time alone.[8]

Adding to that, whereas in 1990 just 3 percent of Americans told Gallup they had no close friends (at work or otherwise),[9] according to the American Survey Center's American Perspectives Survey, by 2021 that number had soared to 12 percent.[10] The decline in social connectedness over this period was particularly marked for young adults, who as of 2020 reported spending 70 percent less time (nearly two hours less per day) with friends compared to in 2003.[11]

At the same time, the share of Americans receiving mental health care increased by a third, with a large portion of that increase occurring between 2018 and 2021.[12] It seems that all of this solitude carries a price.

With so many signs indicating that people are lacking the social connections they need to underpin their well-being, it's become clear that leaders must help them regain it at work.

According to Harvard Medical School professor Dr. Robert Waldinger, coauthor of the massive bestseller *The Good Life: Lessons from the World's Longest Scientific Study of Happiness*:[13] "Good relationships keep us healthier and happier, period. Connection and teamwork aren't necessary just for productivity, but for employee morale as well. A leader's goal, therefore, must be to encourage people to feel part of a community that has a greater purpose."[14]

> *When friends work together, they're more trusting and committed to one another's success. That means they share more information and spend more time helping. . . . They make better choices and get more done.*
>
> —ADAM GRANT, Wharton Business School professor[15]

In a 2023 conversation I had on my *Lead from the Heart* podcast with London Business School professor Herminia Ibarra (author of *Act Like a Leader, Think Like a Leader*[16]), she stressed that when we all worked in offices every day, we couldn't help but interact with our colleagues. In today's hybrid working era, however, those opportunities have been drastically reduced. "Because human beings tend to be narcissistic and lazy," Ibarra explained, "if we're not bumping into people in the hallways and elevator, it's now much harder to connect. So, leaders have to make it more intentional. We can't rely on it happening organically."[17]

What Drives Well-Being

According to Jan-Emmanuel De Neve, director of Oxford University's Well-Being Research Center, when we think about workplace happiness and well-being, the key drivers include the following:

- Feeling appreciated for one's contributions

- Having opportunities to grow and develop

- Having choices about where and when work gets done

- Enjoying feelings of accomplishment

- Having a sense of belonging

- Feeling fairly compensated

- Knowing trust, diversity, and inclusion are valued within one's team and organization

Respondents to De Neve's survey were asked not only to list all of the things that contribute to their sense of belonging at work, but to rank them. Based on the millions of responses, the answer to the question of what drives employee well-being boils down to just two things: *feeling* that their organization and their manager care about them as a human being, and *feeling* that they have colleagues around them who value them as well. And (as was mentioned in this book's Introduction), his research shows that "having a sense of belonging" ranks as the single most important factor of all.[18]

> *We hear that people leave companies mostly because of their manager when, more often, it's because they don't feel appreciated by the people around them.*
>
> —JAN-EMMANUEL DE NEVE[19]

What *Is* Belonging?

According Geoffrey Cohen, Stanford University psychology and organizational behavior professor and author of *Belonging: The Science of Creating Connection and Bridging Divides*, belonging is the feeling that we're part of a larger group that values, respects, and cares for us—and to which we feel we have something to contribute. It's a sense that we're all in this together. "The word 'belong' literally means 'to go with,'" Cohen explains, "and our species has evolved to journey through life with each other. Our desire to be part of a group is 'among the most powerful forces to be found.'" In fact, he notes, "evolutionary biologists argue that being members of a group was essential to our survival and that our species developed a fear of being isolated."[20]

In his book *The Happiness Advantage*, author Shawn Achor equally stresses that social support is by far the greatest predictor of human happiness and well-being, and a source of resilience: "We are more equipped to handle challenges and obstacles when we pool the resources of those around us and capitalize on even the smallest moments we spend interacting with others." Achor also observes that "the better we feel about . . . workplace relationships, the more effective we will be."[21]

Final Thoughts

Perhaps the single most important idea I hope you'll take from this book is that a workplace leader must intentionally create and sustain a relationship-based culture—one that ensures everyone on their team feels they belong in it, are secure in it, and are personally connected to it.

The first step in this process is to find creative ways to bring people together—such as through ongoing team-building activities, volunteering and social events, and casual employee gatherings (ideally during work hours)—simply to foster the communication and interactions that once occurred naturally.

An important second step is to embed team meetings (celebrations, performance recognition events, group learning sessions, team huddles, new employee introductions, and the like) with rituals. That's because regularly scheduled activities and ceremonies elicit feelings of stability. They evoke emotion and contribute greatly to building a united sense of team identity.

French sociologist Émile Durkheim believed that when people participate in rituals of all kinds, a "social electricity" is generated. Because of the feelings of closeness they build, he said, rituals are essential if you seek to foster a sense of community and belonging.[22]

Rituals make communities and cultures tick. They can forge people from different backgrounds together, and make people feel closer to their teammates.

—MICHAEL NORTON,
Harvard Business School professor[23]

Consider starting every monthly meeting by celebrating team achievements, milestones, and employee contributions. Be creative in deciding what special awards or tokens you'll give out for meeting goals and outstanding performance, and maintain those same ones in perpetuity. They don't have to be extravagant. It's the consistency—the ritual—that's important.

Identify behaviors that align with your team's values and mission (e.g., innovation, collaboration, initiative, etc.), and create unique rituals around these behaviors. You can go even further by finding additional clever ways to separately celebrate employees who truly live those values.

Welcome all new employees with the same "welcome package," including personalized items and company swag, and assign them a "buddy" to ensure every new person feels part of the team from day one.

Most rituals will and should develop organically, and by involving your employees in creating other special ceremonies and traditions, you will naturally reinforce your team's cohesion. The great benefit of team rituals is that they help develop a deep sense of camaraderie and togetherness (as if everyone's in on the secret), leading ordinary events to grow into meaningful, *shared* experiences—the kind of experiences that are the cornerstone of human (and therefore employee) well-being.

7

Be a Positive Force

*Positivity opens us. The first core truth about
positive emotions is that they open our hearts and our minds,
making us more receptive and more creative.*

—BARBARA FREDRICKSON[1]

Over the past half century, Dr. John Gottman has studied thousands of married couples, and in the process become one of the world's foremost relationship researchers. He's professor emeritus of psychology at the University of Washington and coauthor of *The Seven Principles for Making Marriage Work*,[2] a book that has sold well over one million copies.

Through his extensive research, Gottman has identified the clear patterns of behavior that distinguish thriving couples from unhappy ones. One remarkable discovery is that what all healthy interpersonal relationships (including marriages) share is a disproportionately high ratio of positive to negative interactions.

According to Gottman, the ideal positivity ratio is 5:1.[3] This means that for each challenging conversation, squabble, or full-on argument a couple will predictably have in their relationship, theirs will remain a stable and happy union if each partner has five (or more) positive interactions to offset it.

Over the years, Gottman has identified a consistent list of positive behaviors that directly contribute to strong and fulfilling relationships. These include showing a partner genuine *interest* (e.g., soliciting their perspective, inquiring about their day), maintaining regular and open *communication*, staying *connected* through phone or text messages while apart, *listening* attentively, *praising* and expressing *appreciation,* working *collaboratively* on shared projects, and using small, regular acts of *kindness* to reinforce how much their partner matters to them.

Other researchers wondered whether Gottman's "magic ratio" might also apply to work relationships—including between workplace managers and their employees. One study published in 2004 evaluated sixty different leadership teams, based on their financial performance, customer satisfaction scores, and feedback from team members.[4] The researchers found that the single most important factor that differentiated high-performing teams from low-performing ones was the ratio of positive to negative interactions employees experienced—between one another, and between themselves and their managers. Their conclusion was that Gottman's ratio applied to these kinds of relationships too, with high-performing work teams maintaining, on average, a 5.6:1 positive to negative ratio.

The clear implication is that in order for interpersonal relationships of any kind to flourish, the people in those relationships must also flourish.

Barbara Fredrickson, professor of psychology and neuroscience at the University of North Carolina at Chapel Hill, developed what she calls the "broaden and build" theory and proved that positive feelings and emotions actually enable human well-being. According to Fredrickson, "The sum of all research on emotions is that people who have plenty of positive emotions in their lives tend to be healthier, more creative, get along well with others, and broaden their awareness, allowing them to see more options when faced with a problem."[5]

Human beings are hardwired to thrive on positive emotions. Human thriving—optimal functioning—is tied to consistently experiencing positive emotions.

—BARBARA FREDRICKSON[6]

Very early in his career, social psychologist Roy Baumeister was unhappy in his job and decided to start tracking the days he felt "good," "bad," and "neutral" at work. Within a few months, his tally showed that the good days outnumbered the bad ones two to one—and that's when he decided to quit.

Baumeister's logic was that it made no sense to stay in a job where he was happy only two-thirds of the time. And this epiphany led him to the realization that human beings experience negative emotions far more powerfully than positive ones. His conclusion was that a 2:1 positivity ratio is unacceptable for most people, whether it be in a job or in a marriage.

Baumeister would later go on to write *The Power of Bad: How the Negativity Effect Rules Us and How We Can Rule It*, where he and coauthor John Tierney cite groundbreaking research that proves the human brain (and heart, apparently) is actually hardwired to react more strongly to negative influences than to positive ones, by a factor of at least four to one.[7]

To illustrate their finding, Baumeister and Tierney drew on the pioneering work of University of Pittsburgh Medical School researcher Robert Schwartz on the effects of positive and negative thinking on mental health. Schwartz's research indicated that:

- "Severely depressed" people tend to have twice as many negative feelings and emotions as positive ones.

- "Mildly dysfunctional" people experience about equal numbers of positive and negative feelings.

- "Normal functioning" people average two and a half positive feelings for every negative one.

- "Optimal functioning" people—those who really flourish—average four or more positive feelings for every negative one.

Based on this, Schwartz concluded that every negative feeling or emotion a person experiences in their daily life is approximately four times as powerful as a positive one. Baumeister and Tierney called this the "Rule of Four."

In Chapter 4, we saw that as leaders, how we make our people feel is the key determinant of employee well-being. The work described here reinforces and builds upon this understanding, by proving that personal and work relationships remain healthy and sustainable only when positive experiences (emotions) consistently outweigh negative ones.

We can't overlook that the C-suite requires workplace managers to enforce company policies, rules, and procedures, to set high expectations and address poor performance, and to implement changes and make decisions that are often unpopular—actions that all have the potential to upset people and induce negative attitudes. Work on its own is often highly demanding, frustrating, stressful, and exhausting. Customers can be rude and difficult, and every manager on the planet will inevitably (even if inadvertently) contribute to employee distress through some decision or action that they take.

The good news is that most employees are resilient and will rebound. They'll take these lumps and remain loyal and committed—just as long as they believe they work for a manager whose positive influence in their lives consistently outweighs the negative.

Being a positive force in leadership has little to do with acting happy all the time or being cloyingly sweet or overly accommodating. What it does require is optimism, enthusiasm, solutions orientation, encouragement, kindness, thoughtfulness, approachability, interest, appreciation, and a search for the good. Positive leaders make us feel as if we matter to them. They encourage open communication and help everyone on their team to feel connected and comfortable sharing their voice. They're intentional about being a positive force.

The science is clear that leaning into positivity directly supports physical, mental, and emotional well-being. And being a positive leader will not only ensure that you maintain healthy and rewarding relationships with those around you; your uplifting energy will also influence them to be your avid supporters.

Final Thoughts

There's a fascinating cognitive bias known as "illusory superiority" that influences us to overestimate our abilities and perceive ourselves as being "better than average" in a wide range of domains, including our intelligence, driving skills, and generosity. Basically, we like to believe we are superior to other people in a lot of ways.

But we can avoid falling into the trap of assuming we're good at something before we've fully confirmed it. Simply go and ask your life partner or a close family member, along with several employees and colleagues, how you might become a more positive influence for them. Are you as positive as you think you are? Where are your gaps? This important exercise will help you find out. Then you can calibrate your behavior to show positivity more often.

8

Turn Over Every Stone

In a world that is constantly changing, there is no one sub-
ject or set of subjects that will serve you for the foreseeable
future, let alone for the rest of your life. The most import-
ant skill to acquire now is learning how to learn.

—JOHN NAISBITT, renowned futurist[1]

Whatever knowledge and expertise we possess today will inevitably be transcended by new discoveries, inventions, innovations,
and technological breakthroughs, possibly rendering some of what we
now know obsolete. That's the essence of John Naisbitt's insight here—
not to mention his warning that, as the world around us is continuously
and rapidly evolving, we'd better evolve too.

We're wise to proactively align ourselves to the speed of change by
embracing lifelong learning, seeking new information, exploring different perspectives, and questioning the status quo. We must remain vigi-
lantly and passionately curious.

The word *curious* means "eager to know or learn," and it's a word we should embrace. Curiosity is the one discipline that can propel us toward the growth and new understanding we will need in order to excel long term in our leadership careers.

Research shows that humans come into the world with a high level of curiosity. Children who exhibit strong curiosity tend to achieve higher intelligence scores compared to their less curious peers,[2] and studies confirm that curiosity enhances empathy, improves learning, and leads to better problem solving.[3]

But something insidious often happens when people become adults. We become almost anti-curious.

One big reason for this is that our human egos prefer to feel knowledgeable and successful at all times. Not wanting to feel vulnerable to anything unknown or in flux, our minds silence otherwise solid reasons to seek new methods, approaches, or skills. "You're already doing great," our egos assure us. "There's no need to invest time and energy in anything new."

Our egos are really conniving in this regard. Who wouldn't prefer to rest on their laurels and enjoy their achievements rather than take a class, read a book, earn a credential, solicit other viewpoints, or otherwise put in the hard work required to keep their skills and mastery current?

Most of us greatly underestimate how effective our egos can be at puffing us up and luring us away from curiosity-driven behavior. As London Business School professor Gary Hamel observes, leaders are so certain that we're already excelling in our jobs, it's led us to being unreasonably sure of ourselves: "As human beings, we tend to overestimate our abilities and underestimate our faults. In one survey, 84 percent of middle managers and 97 percent of executives claimed to be among the top 10 percent of performers in their organization."[4]

Another pernicious reason many people steer clear of being curious has to do with what cognitive psychologist Peter Wason named "confirmation bias": the perverse human tendency to disregard information that doesn't confirm or strengthen our existing beliefs and values.

The human understanding when it has once
adopted an opinion (either as being the received opinion
or as being agreeable to itself) draws all things else
to support and agree with it.

—SIR FRANCIS BACON, 17th century philosopher[5]

Inherently, confirmation bias greatly narrows our focus. Far worse, it prevents us from exploring alternative or diverse viewpoints—or even considering other possibilities altogether. With respect to leadership, the human inclination to confirm our views rather than challenge them by exploring other perspectives is the greatest curiosity killer there is. It prevents us from asking ourselves: *What might I be missing? What can I learn here? Could I be wrong?*

If you've ever been in a meeting where someone was sharing new or unfamiliar information, you've surely heard your ego's voice urging you to keep quiet and not ask questions. Not wanting to appear ignorant, weak, or incompetent in front of others, our egos tamp down our curiosity and deprive us of the discovery we need. Yet ironically, in their book *A Curious Mind: The Secret to a Bigger Life*, Brian Grazer and Charles Fishman reveal that the people who ask the most questions in workplace meetings typically come across as the smartest people in the room![6]

I've gone from believing that if you ask questions,
it meant you're fundamentally not smart, to
believing that the more you ask, the more curious
you are, the smarter you get.

—TIM COOK, Apple CEO[7]

If we are to become ever curious, ever growing, and ever evolving, we must cultivate vigilance. We must strengthen our inner discipline to ignore our mind's pleadings and make ourselves open to critical feedback, to taking risks, to trying new things, and to hearing widely divergent views from our own.

Our motto from this day forward must be: "Less certainty, more inquiry." Only the person who listens continues to learn. Those who believe they know everything learn nothing.

The Power of Listening

In her book *The Power of Onlyness*, Nilofer Merchant reports that "Forty percent of the variance in what makes someone a good leader is tied to listening. That's the single biggest variance other than basic competence. Other research says the average person listens at only 25 percent effectiveness."[8]

One big problem when it comes to listening is that our devices are always close by, tempting us to look down or vibrating in our pockets. We're easily distracted, and we often feel rushed or impatient while listening to other people speaking.

When someone else is talking, some of us have an urge to interject our own experiences, sometimes interrupting the other person. If we truly commit ourselves to curiosity, then we must commit equally to listening to what others have to say. As Rick Rubin says, "To listen impatiently is to hear nothing at all."[9]

The best way to invite honesty and earn trust with people is to demonstrate interest in them. When we are fully present, we influence others to open up, share their true feelings, and, notably, give us the valuable information we need. This, of course, requires that we first be curious.

In 2013, I spent the day at Google's Silicon Valley headquarters with the organization's rather forward-thinking talent management team. I learned more about the importance of leadership curiosity that day than I had over my entire career—especially with respect to how a leader's curiosity builds trust, boosts employee satisfaction, and bolsters well-being.

Karen May, then vice president of people development at Google, told me that the company's leaders credited their curiosity about employees' thinking as one of the greatest drivers of Google's success: "If you value your employees, and you really care about them as whole people, one thing you do is give them voice and really listen."

Google routinely solicited employees' feedback on everything from how they wanted their compensation to how Google should design the branded bicycles used on its campuses. Managers also learned to pepper people with questions like "What do you think?" and "How might we do this?"

"It creates a different kind of experience being here," May explained, "and also then creates opportunities for us in what we try to solve together."

Google's brilliant example demonstrates that when we create a culture of curiosity within our teams, we inherently encourage employees to participate actively in discussions, projects, and problem solving. This makes them feel more involved, integral to the organization, and safe in expressing their ideas. And by turning over every stone and encouraging others to do the same, we as managers naturally create a more adaptable, collaborative, and resilient workforce, all of which greatly fortifies well-being.

Get Out of Your Shell

One more highly effective way of being curious is to take on as many new projects, assignments, challenges, and experiences at work as you possibly can. As Herminia Ibarra observes, "It's in doing that we learn most and grow. I've seen this motivation in the very best leaders I've worked with—but it requires a willingness to struggle, fail, and live in the discomfort of not knowing everything. Too many managers spend most days doing what they do well at the expense of taking on assignments where they will learn new things."[10]

In surveying her many MBA students at the London Business School over the years, Ibarra found that the majority of them let the routine and operational aspects of their jobs consume too much of their time[11]—perhaps due to their egos' insistence on staying within their comfort zones, we might wonder?

Final Thoughts

Curiosity isn't just about acquiring facts; it's about embracing wonder, staying open-minded, and seeking new understanding.

Next time you're in a book store (brick-and-mortar or online) and see a title that interests you, buy it and read it—especially if it's in a genre outside your normal interests. Reading fiction and nonfiction alike will expose you to different viewpoints, cultures, and themes. Every book you open will provide a unique lens through which you can see the world from new and varied angles.

Listening to audio books is just as valuable. So, too, is listening to podcasts—again, across topics and areas of interest. Take a moment to consider all the ways you can open yourself to acquiring new information, challenge your own knowledge and beliefs, and commit to creating spaces for others to explore as well.

Curious-minded leaders know that they and their people can never stop learning—and, more importantly, they never should.

9

Step into the Fog

Accept Uncertainty and Ambiguity

*The universe is not required to be in
perfect harmony with human ambition.*

—CARL SAGAN[1]

W hen it comes to just about any important project or event in our
lives, most of us prefer to have a great sense of control over the
outcomes. Meticulous planning helps us mentally prepare and assure
ourselves that things will play out just as we intend.

The problem (which proves very hard for us humans to accept) is
that no matter how many safeguards we put into our plans—and no matter how certain we are of those plans—there are simply no guarantees
that life will unfold as we expect.

Our control over outcomes has always been a complete illusion.
Planes don't always take off on time, important deadlines get missed,
brides and grooms change their minds moments before weddings, sum-
mer vacations get wiped out by rain, and the stock market goes down.

Yet, so powerful is our need to feel in control that whenever life fails to conform to our expectations, we instinctively treat it like a violation from the universe. When a traffic jam makes us late for a meeting, a client postpones a purchase, a top employee quits, a goal isn't met—even when a sports team we root for doesn't win—our human tendency is to feel like a victim. We get frustrated and angry, and shake our fists at the heavens for failing to follow our internal script.

At issue here is that all of our venting, sulking, cursing, blaming—even berating ourselves for our setbacks—ignores the reality that insecurity and unpredictability are woven into our existence. And all the energy and time we devote to brooding over and resenting our negative experiences needlessly delays us from conceding to reality as it is and directly addressing our problems.

A far more enlightened, powerful, realistic, and mature way of approaching life and leadership, therefore, is to fully accept that our destinies are *never* certain. That's not to say we should ever stop planning, analyzing, strategizing, and the like—we must, of course, always do our very best to align our preparations and actions to what we know and believe at the time.

It's just that we must recognize that it's entirely counterproductive to react with surprise, anger, or rage when we're met with setbacks, detours, or delays. Instead, we must fully expect that some suboptimal outcomes will occur, despite all our best efforts at preventing them.

Note that once we deeply internalize that results are never entirely in our hands, our worldview profoundly and permanently changes. Tied to the mantra "I accept what is," we become more flexible, poised, and agile—instantly able to soberly and mindfully determine our next best moves. And it's when we're in this exact state that we operate out of the full essence of well-being.

Remembering that we're all human, it's entirely unrealistic to think we won't ever again feel disappointment and distress when our plans and goals go awry. But our key objective in these situations must be to avoid being emotionally triggered by them, or allowing ourselves to be undermined by panic and apprehension.

Truth be told, the human ego so greatly desires a world it can predict that it floods us with fear whenever a problem occurs—it wants us to believe the trouble we're in will lead to our demise.

Knowing the dark and insidious ways our mind seeks to maintain control, we must prepare ourselves to tune out its undermining influence and to move forward with courage and self-confidence. When we're able to step back into a state of calm and invest time in creating thoughtful and innovative solutions to our problems, we build a rare leadership mastery for sailing through rough waters with resilience and adaptability.

Whereas "uncertainty" generally refers to situations where we face an unpredictable future, "ambiguity" arises when we're presented with multiple options and there's no clear right or wrong one for us to choose.

While we might imagine that leading a team of people through an ambiguous dilemma will be even more challenging than maneuvering through any kind of uncertainty, a mind that's been trained to anticipate unpredictable outcomes is well on its way toward maintaining composure and equanimity in even the hairiest of situations. In other words, being comfortable with uncertainty equips us to successfully and calmly navigate ambiguity.

As the Drucker Institute's Rick Wartzman and Kelly Tang note in their article "The Key to Being a Successful Leader? It's Adaptability," companies that are led by those who are tolerant of ambiguity and are adaptable tend to score highest on Drucker's gauge of corporate effectiveness. "Having to interpret vague or contradictory signals and being forced to continually transform a business," they observe, "'would overwhelm or exhaust a lot of people. . . . But it energizes others. These leaders have a fearlessness.'"[2]

As these findings suggest, the world we live in today will absolutely crush managers who cling to a need for structure, detail, and exactitude.

Being comfortable with haziness and reacting with nimbleness . . . are the most prominent hallmarks of being an effective leader in our turbulent times.

—RICK WARTZMAN AND KELLY TANG[3]

Final Thoughts

To make management decisions when your certainty over the outcome is low—or lower than you'd prefer—you'll need both courage and a willingness to accept some discomfort.

You may need some time to build up a stomach for this, so your goal should be to incrementally evolve your ability to make choices in situations where you have less data and certainty than you'd like.

Over the coming weeks and months, whenever you are faced with an important decision to make, ask yourself these two questions:

On a scale of one to ten, how certain do I feel about this outcome?

On a scale of one to ten, how comfortable do I feel about making this decision?

The purpose of this exercise is to reflect upon the gap between your level of certainty and your level of comfort in making the decision—and to challenge yourself to become more at ease with having less certainty and still moving forward.

No one wants to make a decision that could backfire on them, embarrass them, or cost them their job, but deliberately delaying important decisions may actually have even greater downsides. If you're a leader, you will surely fail by being indecisive.

Long before Amazon.com became one of the world's most dominant brands, its founder, Jeff Bezos, explained to his shareholders that being decisive was not only going to be a cornerstone of his leadership philosophy, but that he'd also come to understand that most decisions that lead to bad outcomes can actually be reversed:

> Some decisions are consequential and irreversible or nearly irreversible—one-way doors—and these decisions must be made methodically, carefully, slowly, with great deliberation and consultation. If you walk through and don't like what you see on the other side, you can't get back to where you were before. We can call these Type 1 decisions. But most decisions aren't like that—they are changeable, reversible—they're two-way doors. If you've

made a suboptimal Type 2 decision, you don't have to live with the consequences for that long. You can reopen the door and go back through. Type 2 decisions can and should be made quickly by high judgment individuals or small groups.[4]

The takeaway here is that most decisions we make as managers are "Type 2" and don't carry dire consequences if they don't deliver on our expectations. While highly effective leaders cultivate an ability to comfortably make decisions (often anchored to their personal credo) when the potential outcomes are uncertain or ambiguous, they also possess the courage to promptly unmake them when they determine their original choices didn't work out.

This is a truly powerful leadership perspective that yields great benefits for managers and their employees alike.

Embracing uncertainty as managers fosters a culture of psychological safety, where mistakes are seen as opportunities for growth rather than reasons for punishment. This approach encourages employees to experiment, take reasonable risks, and innovate, knowing that their efforts to learn new skills and find creative solutions are supported. Ultimately, this environment boosts employee well-being by reducing fear of failure and promoting continuous personal and professional development.

Through our own displays of grace under pressure, we directly convey to our teams that any time they face a problem or challenge, it will best be solved by remaining adaptable, patient, and resilient—and by remembering that this is just the way life goes some times.

We're always living in a state of uncertainty—two years ago, two years from now—therefore, part of our challenge as I see it is to make uncertainty . . . our home.

—PICO IYER[5]

10

Loosen Your Grip

Let people own their work and make their own choices—
they'll show you results you didn't think were possible.

—LASZLO BOCK[1]

Since 1967, Sir Michael Marmot, professor of epidemiology and public health at University College London, has been monitoring the health of nearly 30,000 workers at Whitehall, the citadel of Great Britain's civil service.

Seeking to determine whether professional rank influences workplace stress and well-being, Marmot found Whitehall ideal for his study because all of the subjects worked in the same physical environment and in jobs ranked in a precise hierarchy. In other words, few variables affected Whitehall employees other than their rank.

In light of Shakespeare's enduring observation, "uneasy lies the head that wears a crown,"[2] we might assume that people in positions of greater responsibility—those highest up in an organization—would experience more workplace stress.

Surprisingly, Marmot's research conclusively proved the opposite.[3]

Instead, he discovered that lower-ranking workers experience more serious stress-related consequences. They're far more likely to suffer from heart disease and weak immune systems, and their life expectancy is well below average. In the Whitehall study, people in the lowest job grade (e.g., messengers and doorkeepers) had mortality rates three times higher than those in the highest administrative ranks.

Marmot's discovery confirmed that job stress is directly and linearly correlated to position on the company organization chart—the higher our level of responsibility, the lower our job stress.

How Is This Possible?

According to Marmot, the explanation is simple: people whose jobs rank lowest tend to have the least amount of control over their workday lives. Control at work is directly related to one's rung on the organizational ladder—and a lack of control over *how* one's work is performed, and even *when* it gets performed, increases the amount of stress people experience, which undermines their health and well-being.

Importantly, Marmot's research also led him to identify the antidote to workplace stress: give employees more flexibility and control in their jobs and help them flourish.

The Whitehall study revealed that when workers were empowered to contribute more autonomously, given a greater say in work decisions, and allowed more flexibility in their workdays, illness rates decreased. In Marmot's words, "Give people more involvement in their work, more say in what they're doing, more reward for the amount of effort they put out, and it might well be you'll not only have a healthier workplace, but a more productive one as well."[4]

Another remarkable insight from the Whitehall study underscores the overarching themes of this book: by taking measures to improve the well-being of others, we naturally increase our own. Marmot concluded that being compassionate and caring for others are the most important factors in promoting our own longevity.

Connecting with and helping others leads us to living longer, happier, and healthier lives.

How to Give Employees More Control

There is one obvious hurdle that managers must get over in order to feel comfortable allowing their people to perform their jobs with greater freedom and flexibility. They first must learn how to counteract a very legitimate fear: that their employees will end up underperforming, underachieving, and not meeting their goals if they stop being a hands-on or micromanaging supervisor.

The good news is that managers can help themselves and their employees overcome such fears by taking these steps:

Communicate clear goals and expectations.
Studies routinely show that many workers aren't sure of what's expected of them at work—a sign that some managers never slow down enough to establish clear and measurable objectives for their people. But when workers know exactly what's expected of them—and ideally have it communicated to them in writing—they're able to manage their time and assignments more effectively.

Learn to trust.
It's a fatal flaw for managers to believe that employees won't work hard or be effective unless they're closely monitored or even micromanaged. The more informed belief is that the true measure of a leader is how well their teams perform when they aren't around. Effective leadership isn't about overseeing every task personally; it's about creating a team capable of performing well independently.

To achieve this, you need to have trust and confidence in your people. If you struggle with this, start small. Delegate smaller tasks initially, and then gradually increase responsibility as trust is built. You must always ensure, of course, that employees are sufficiently trained to work more independently. Once they are, be certain they know they are accountable for results, not just processes.

Measure performance and routinely share metrics.

Employees need to know where they stand at all times, and this means having access to frequent reports on their progress and outcomes. As London Business School professor Gary Hamel explains, "People can't be self-managing without information. . . . The goal is to provide staffers with all the information they need to monitor their work and make wise decisions."[5]

Be flexible with when and where employees do their work.

Small accommodations, such as allowing a parent to start work later so they can take their child to school in the morning or letting an employee work from home when they need to wait for a plumber to arrive, can make a huge difference in people's lives. When employees are held accountable for results, and you trust them to perform, flexibility here carries little downside and can provide a great boost to their well-being.

Schedule weekly check-ins.

In their book *Nine Lies about Work*, Ashley Goodall and Marcus Buckingham argue that a manager's span of control (i.e., how many people they can effectively supervise) should be determined by how many employees they can meet with *every week* for a thirty-minute check-in.[6] Their point is that managers must routinely touch base with their people to see how they're feeling—while also using that time to discuss their progress, challenges, and needed support.

The objective is to keep everyone aligned to their goals without being overbearing. An added benefit is that you, as the manager, will always be in the loop.

Final Thoughts

Sir Michael Marmot's groundbreaking Whitehall study highlights a vital leadership truth: empowering employees isn't just a nice-to-have, it's a necessity for both well-being and productivity. When managers loosen their grip, by fostering trust and setting clear expectations, they create a thriving work environment where employees are not only healthier, but also more committed and effective. Embrace flexibility and autonomy, and you'll cultivate a team that not only thrives, but also excels.

11

We Instead of Me

Great things in business are never done by
one person; they're done by a team of people.

—STEVE JOBS[1]

According to University of California, Berkeley, psychology professor Dacher Keltner, author of *Born to Be Good: The Science of a Meaningful Life*, the science of altruism and cooperation has found that when teams of people are highly cooperative and other-oriented, they perform better and their organizations are healthier.[2]

Leaders who purposefully foster collaboration and mutual support unleash their teams' full potential. Paraphrasing Aesop, "In union there is strength."

To some managers, an emphasis on teamwork may seem blatantly obvious. But in reality, workplace leaders—notably in sales organizations—often stress internal competition as a means of driving productivity. Additionally, traditional employee performance appraisals tend to be comparative by design, and systematically grade people in relation to their peers.

The unintended consequences of these schemes are that "star" performers routinely end up receiving the majority of the recognition and rewards, and employees learn to compete against each other rather than working cooperatively toward achieving common goals.

Microsoft Then and Now

Nowhere has this been better illustrated than when Steve Ballmer was CEO at Microsoft from 2000 to 2014.

Fiercely believing that his organization's productivity would be elevated through internal competition, Ballmer introduced an employee evaluation system known as "stack ranking."[3]

Every six months, he required managers to rate their employees' performance and assign each of them into one of the following fixed categories:

Top performers: 20 percent of employees

Good performers: 70 percent of employees

Low performers: 10 percent of employees

This meant that even when a team was exceeding all of its targets and goals, only one in five team members could ever be deemed to be excelling. The rigidity of the system meant that solidly contributing employees were forced into buckets that made them unfairly ineligible for salary increases, bonuses, stock awards, and promotions—and Microsoft generally fired anyone graded a low performer.

While the stack ranking system remained in place for many years, Ballmer's methodology quickly proved to have poisonous effects on organizational culture and morale. For starters, it absolutely killed teamwork and innovation. And rather than inspiring people to perform at their best, it routinely marinated them in fear. In a nutshell, it created the antithesis of well-being. According to Kurt Eichenwald, who published an analysis of the company's "cannibalistic" culture in *Vanity*

Fair, "Every current and former Microsoft employee I interviewed—*every one*—cited stack ranking as the most destructive process inside of Microsoft, something that drove out untold numbers of employees."[4]

People simply didn't want to compete every day with colleagues they depended upon.

What's apparent is that the CEO of one of the world's largest companies strongly believed that his job was to build a team of all-stars (by repeatedly firing the "weakest" employees) instead of cultivating a thriving, cohesive organization. But the result of creating a work environment where few people felt supported by those around them was that the high performers, ironically, proved to be the first ones to leave.

The lesson to be taken from Microsoft's stack ranking era is that a manager's job isn't to root out and terminate low performers. Instead, it's to hire well, and then create an environment where talented people can flourish, produce, and sustainably achieve *together*.

Of course, managers will always have some workers who underperform or don't fit in. But while addressing these instances through conversation, coaching, and counseling will always be among their responsibilities, it must not become their primary one.

After Ballmer retired, Microsoft's new CEO, Satya Nadella, and Chief People Officer Kathleen Hogan almost immediately scrapped the stack ranking system. Instead of comparing employees *against* each other, the new review process they created emphasizes three factors: individual impact, how people contribute to their coworkers' success, and how they leverage one another's work. In other words, today, Microsoft's performance evaluations intentionally focus on how much people contribute to their teams.

What Nadella and Hogan clearly understood in their design was that collaboration, mutual trust, and cooperation are crucial to developing new technologies and to achieving virtually every important organizational goal. In addition, the new employee review process no longer limits how many people can earn a high grade. This, of course, means employees are not motivated to undermine colleagues' work in order to shore up their own chances of making the cut.

Not only do we have clear evidence that rivalries of all kinds undermine organizational effectiveness, but cooperation is very much in human DNA—and has helped ensure our species survived when so many others didn't.

According to Harvard Business School professor Rosabeth Moss Kanter, all great coaches in collegiate and professional sports knowingly create cultures of initiative and achievement, with a special emphasis on collaboration. She quotes Joe Banner, who at the time was the president of the Philadelphia Eagles, as saying, "The skill of an athlete is irrelevant until the right culture surrounds them." Three-time Super Bowl winning coach Andy Reid echoed the sentiment: "We preach team. Team, team, team, team, team."[5]

In his book *The Culture Code: The Secrets of Highly Effective Groups*, Daniel Coyle emphasizes that top coaches are also highly disciplined when it comes to the kinds of players they want playing for them.[6] Consistently, he says, they don't merely sign the best athletes they can find; they specifically go after players who have a demonstrated interest in contributing to something bigger than their own careers.

"When you ask people inside highly successful groups to describe their relationship with one another," Coyle observes, "they all tend to choose the same word. This word is not friends or team or tribe or any other equally plausible term. The word they use is family." He quotes IDEO Design's Duane Bray as describing the feeling like this: "Being a familial group . . . allows you to take more risks, give each other permission, and have moments of vulnerability that you could never have in a more normal setting."[7]

Coyle also describes how, in the 1990s, sociologists James Baron and Michael Hannan analyzed the founding cultures of nearly two hundred Silicon Valley startups and found that most followed one of three basic models:

- The star model, focused on finding and hiring the best people

- The professional model, focused on building the group around specific skill sets

- The commitment model, focused on developing a group with shared values and strong emotional bonds

Not surprisingly, the commitment model consistently led to the highest rates of success.

And what's the mantra of teams like this?

We all depend on each other for our success and our well-being.

Final Thoughts

Take some time to consider how much you emphasize collaboration and teamwork in your leadership today.

Do you tend to spotlight individual achievements more often than group successes?

Do you prefer to hire people who strive for personal accomplishments, or people with a history of being synergistic?

Do you believe all of your team's members are invested in its success?

Do your employees instinctively come to the aid of a struggling coworker, or are they more likely to let them work things out on their own?

Would your employees describe themselves as being a "family"—or at least "united"—as Daniel Coyle mentions?

When you prioritize teamwork, make it a cornerstone of your leadership philosophy, and celebrate it whenever you see it on display; you'll end up building extraordinary trust and camaraderie among your team—and you'll all reap the benefits.

12

Growth Creates Happiness

Maximize Employee Potential

Happiness is neither virtue nor pleasure nor
this thing nor that but simply growth. We are
happy when we are growing.

—JOHN BUTLER YEATS[1]

One of my earliest college assignments was to write a paper on John Steinbeck's classic book, *The Grapes of Wrath*. I had high hopes of earning a degree in English literature at the time, and I knew my performance in this Twentieth Century Novel class would clarify my readiness for the demanding curriculum.

The paper I wrote didn't even merit a grade. Indeed, it fell so far short of my professor's minimum expectations that she insisted I rewrite it entirely.

When I met with her in her office to discuss the situation, she sternly told me that my work was a complete mess and that the standards at this top university were much higher than what previously had been expected of me. She used words like "wild" and "undisciplined" to describe my writing. To drive her point home, she said it would be a "Herculean" task for me to write a second paper good enough to earn a proper grade.

It was a stunning blow. My professor's feedback was crushing, demoralizing—and confirming of what I'd deeply feared: I couldn't cut it.

She could have chosen to leave it at that and wait and see if I would rewrite the paper, or drop out of her class entirely. But just when I thought our conversation was over, she said, "Mr. Crowley, as unacceptable as this paper is, I see a cleverness and originality in you. If you're willing to work hard, I think you have the potential to be a good writer."

Potential?

That one word was deeply heartening, because it instantly reset my own self-assessment. This wasn't a fatal failure; it was only a setback. That final statement implied that my educational dreams weren't out of reach at all—as I long as I was committed to doing the work needed to improve my skills. In other words, rather than leave me dejected and motivated to quit, my professor chose to inspire me by saying that *she* believed I had a potential for growth lying deep inside me.

As you might imagine, this brief interaction proved to be a transformational moment in my life. On the spot, I fully committed myself to the journey of becoming an effective writer, and to never again doubting my ability to earn my literature degree.

The truth is that many of us greatly underestimate our talents and potential for growth. We're under the illusion that we're somehow limited and flawed—which prevents us from seeing how powerful and capable we really are. And, sadly, this keeps too many of us from ever fulfilling our full human promise.

Most people live . . . in a very restricted circle of their potential being. They make use of a very small portion of their possible consciousness, and of their soul's resources in general, much like a [person] who, out of [their] whole bodily organism, should get into a habit of using and moving only [their] little finger.

—WILLIAM JAMES, father of American psychology[2]

Consider for a moment all the people you work with—colleagues on your team, especially—and ask yourself how many of them you believe have far more capability, creativity, and talent than they presently utilize in their jobs. How many would you say are filled with far greater potential? If James is correct, the answer you came up with was most, if not all, of them.

To be an enlightened leader today is to understand that the limits of human potential are mostly imagined. Self-doubt is part of the human condition, and a manager's job is to open people's eyes to their own hidden genius. It's also their role to help employees become who they are truly capable of becoming. As former US First Lady Rosalynn Carter famously said, "A leader takes people where they want to go. A great leader takes people where they don't necessarily want to go, but ought to go."[3]

During the course of my career, I became the manager of several different teams when the previous managers were retiring, leaving the firm, or otherwise moving on to other assignments.

Each time, I met in advance with the departing manager just to get the lay of the land, and to learn about the people I was inheriting. In *every instance*, the manager intentionally sought to convince me that certain employees were "maxed out" and couldn't be expected to contribute beyond their current mediocre levels of performance.

But, just as you might imagine, as I began working with all of the people previous managers had left for dead, I found they hadn't reached the limits of their abilities at all. They just needed someone to identify their talents, challenge them, direct them, coach them, encourage them—and believe in them in the same way my professor had done for me.

The lesson here is to never place limits on human potential. As managers, we must not put people in boxes or pigeonhole them. Our job is to judge effort, initiative, and performance—not what we think is in someone's heart.

We also must never be selective about whose potential we choose to develop. It's long been common practice in organizations to identify the crème de la crème of employees—people deemed to be "high talent" *and* "high potential"—and to give those people the lion's share of the development opportunities. One reason alone justifies growing everyone, and not just a select few: the benefits to leaders and organizations are huge when we help people perform at levels previously believed to be unreachable.

On top of that, in order for teams to flourish, everyone must feel they are growing in some meaningful way. When we feel we are learning, we feel more competent and more confident that we are progressing. Becoming more over time is a crucial component of well-being, not to mention of a happy and fulfilling life.

To Grow People, We Must First Believe They *Can* Grow

In 2006, Stanford University professor Carol Dweck published her now classic book *Mindset: The New Psychology of Success*.[4] In it, she explained that people tend to believe one of two things about human intelligence and abilities: either they're largely fixed, or they can be developed. "Fixed mindset" beliefs assert that people either have it or they don't (i.e., some people are smart and others aren't), whereas "growth mindset" beliefs suggest human aptitude can be expanded through hard work and support from others.

Dweck's research showed that adopting a growth mindset can lead to greater success and fulfillment in various aspects of life. It fosters a love for learning, resilience in the face of obstacles, and a belief in the potential for growth and improvement. In contrast, a fixed mindset proves to hinder progress and create a fear of failure that limits opportunities.

Around the time *Mindset* was published, Mary C. Murphy, one of Dweck's PhD students, proposed that the dominant mindset in an individual's work environment would likely play an even more significant role in shaping their self-conception than their personal mindset (a thesis embraced by Dweck).

Murphy went on to spend over a decade researching how mindsets operate at group and organizational levels. She identified two general types of workplace cultures, depending on whether a growth or a fixed mindset dominates in a team or organization. Workplaces with what Murphy calls a "Culture of Growth" believe in and value all people's abilities and potential. In contrast, in workplaces with a "Culture of Genius," it is generally believed that only some people have significant talent and aptitude to leverage, while others (permanently) have less of it.

According to Murphy, "A growth mindset culture is one that values, fosters, and rewards growth and development among all members"—and such a culture is strongly associated with greater employee well-being. "In our analysis," she reports, "employees of organizations with strong Cultures of Genius were 40 percent less satisfied with the company's culture compared with those who worked for organizations with strong Cultures of Growth."[5]

Organizations and teams that hold a growth mindset and infuse their policies and practices with it have employees who are more motivated and committed, more mutually supportive, and more creative and innovative.

—CAROL DWECK,
in her foreword to Mary Murphy's *Cultures of Growth*[6]

Word to the wise: we feel most alive—with increased well-being—when we are learning new things—especially when someone sees our potential and wants us to develop further.

See Yourself More as a Coach and Less as a Manager

Nearly a decade ago, when Gallup and other organizations began publishing research on how to most effectively manage Gen Y employees (people born between 1980 and 1996) who were just entering the workplace, one of the key discoveries was that "millennials" generally didn't want to have a manager at all; they wanted a coach.[7]

Ever since, I've strongly believed that workplace leaders should not only self-identify as being more of a coach than a manager, they should dedicate more of their time to coaching than to managing.

In a 2023 conversation I had on my *Lead from the Heart* podcast with London Business School professor Herminia Ibarra (author of *Act Like a Leader, Think Like a Leader*, mentioned in Chapter 6), I made this exact point—and she brilliantly explained why coaching hasn't become a more common practice in our workplaces. She first cited *Emotional Intelligence* author Daniel Goleman's classic study on leadership styles, where leaders ranked "coaching" as their least favorite style.[8] The common complaint was that managers simply didn't have time for the "slow and tedious" work of teaching people and helping them grow.

But the plain-speaking Ibarra told me she believed this was all just an excuse: "We imagine coaching is too painful because we're not skilled at it. Coaching is helping people achieve their potential. And once we get skilled at it—by doing it more regularly—we can do it more quickly and see the benefits of it. The best way to become a good coach is to coach. At the beginning, tell people you're working on this new skill set, want to help them develop—and may not always get it right."[9]

In their book *Nine Lies about Work*, Marcus Buckingham and Ashley Goodall reiterate the need for managers to dedicate time every week to coaching their people. The primary reason they are so insistent that coaching be done this faithfully is that frequency proves to be more important than quality. People don't actually want or need detailed direction all the time; often, they just want to know they are on track, and to hear it confirmed by their boss. This investment pays dividends—as Buckingham and Goodall observe, "The data reveals . . . that those team leaders who check in every week with every team member have higher levels of engagement and performance, and lower levels of voluntary turnover."[10]

> *Thirty minutes is all it takes to provide recognition,*
> *review work priorities, and—most importantly—*
> *offer guidance and support.*
>
> —MARCUS BUCKINGHAM[11]

In his massive bestseller *The Coaching Habit: Say Less, Ask More & Change the Way You Lead Forever*, Michael Bungay Stanier also emphasizes that coaching needn't require a huge time commitment or always be complex.[12] As a means to surfacing the topics most important to employees, Bungay Stanier recommends managers initiate coaching conversations with simple, straightforward questions like: "What's on your mind?" "And what else?" He stresses that a lot of coaching discussions should be devoted to empowering people to find their own answers. His follow-up questions include "What's the real challenge here for you?" and "What [outcome] do you want?"

"How can I help?" comes later.

In his 2024 book *10 to 25: The Science of Motivating Young People*, University of Texas at Austin professor David Yeager asserts that it's not just millennial workers who want and need to be coached regularly.[13] His research highlights that Gen Z workers also respond better to coaching and mentoring, because it aligns with their developmental needs for status and respect. As Yeager explains it, from around age ten and up to age twenty-five, young people start craving socially rewarding experiences and become highly sensitive to social pain. Coaching and mentoring provide the validation, respect, and support they need, which helps them feel valued and motivated.

And once again, Yeager dispels the misconception that mentoring is time-consuming. On the contrary, he argues that it saves time in the long run by creating a more autonomous and motivated workforce.

Final Thoughts

According to Liz Wiseman in her book with Greg McKeown *Multipliers: How the Best Leaders Make Everyone Smarter*, managers who purposely optimize their talent get two times more out of people.[14] This is yet more confirmation that when we focus on supporting employee well-being, elevated team performance comes as our reward.

The next time you meet with the members of your team, ask them individually what they would like to do and learn next—and how you can help them accomplish it. Tapping into what you know of their talents and interests, be prepared to propose a few ideas of your own.

And never forget Shakespeare's discerning insight into the human condition: "We know what we are, but know not what we may be."[15]

13

Care About— Even Love— Your People

The most important thing in good leadership is truly caring. The best leaders in any profession care about the people they lead, and the people who are being led know when the caring is genuine and when it's faked or not there at all.

—DEAN SMITH, Hall of Fame coach[1]

When Dean Smith retired after thirty-six seasons as head coach of the men's basketball team at the University of North Carolina, Chapel Hill, he was the most successful collegiate basketball coach in United States history. As well as leading an American men's basketball team to an Olympic gold medal, his teams had won three national championships—and over 95 percent of his players had earned their college degrees.[2]

After he retired, Smith went on to write *The Carolina Way: Leadership Lessons from a Life in Coaching*, where he documented the values he believed most influenced his remarkable leadership success—popularly summarized as, among others, "stay humble, stay hungry," "act with honor and integrity," "lead by example," and "never underestimate teamwork."[3]

But in his book, and in numerous interviews, Smith insisted he excelled as a coach mostly because he loved his players, and made each one feel they mattered to him personally. Smith didn't just teach his young players how to win on the basketball court; he purposefully taught them how to excel in life.

It's a funny thing that we respond so strongly to stories about deeply caring sports coaches like Dean Smith, yet instinctively feel that workplace managers should lead impersonally—certainly without any kind of affection or regard for their employees or their overall well-being.

What every workplace manager needs to know is that caring for the people they lead is not soft, weak, or antithetical to driving performance. As Smith's words imply, whenever human beings—in any setting—feel that their leader *genuinely* cares about them, it becomes an emotional catalyst for them to contribute more, not less.

As University of California, Berkeley, social scientist Dacher Keltner says in his book *The Power Paradox: How We Gain and Lose Influence*, "We have a deep cultural intuition that nice guys finish last, that one must step on others to rise in the ranks. . . . But nothing could [be] further from the truth."[4] We no longer earn power by being self-focused, but by consistently acting in ways that improve the lives of others. Power is expressed in advocacy, compassion, respect, attentiveness to human feelings, and gratitude toward others.

Caring wins games—and it also wins in business.

From Gallup and others, we have learned that an employee's relationship with their manager is the top factor in determining their satisfaction and well-being at work.[5] Research also confirms that the most effective workplace leaders "build caring and respectful relationships to strengthen their team's performance"—the problem is that less than one in five American workers say their manager makes that kind of investment in them.[6]

What's become irrefutable is that people today want to work for a boss who prioritizes their success, growth, and well-being; someone who is their advocate and coach. And apparently, far too few managers today are either hardwired or currently motivated to lead this way.

In his essay "Schopenhauer as Educator," Friedrich Nietzsche states that there are many paths to be taken in life, and that it's entirely up to each of us to determine which path is our right one.[7] Nietzsche implies most people aren't willing to do the hard work that's required to identify their true self—nor do they have the courage and strength to take the right path once it's known to them. But for those daring few who truly want to do so, he says the way to discover what they were put on this earth to do is to review their past experiences, identify all the times they felt most fulfilled, and then see if there are clear consistencies.

The challenge to us as workplace managers today is to complete Nietzsche's exercise for the purpose of confirming whether or not leading a team of human beings is what truly makes our own hearts sing. If our greatest joys and satisfaction prove to have routinely come from personal achievements, it's a sign that we'll end up competing with—or simply being indifferent to—all of the people we manage, rather than being their champions. And competing with our employees for recognition, status, and career growth is simply managerial malpractice.

So, ask yourself this question: *Knowing everything I know about what makes workplace managers successful, is leading people fully aligned to who I am at my core?*

If your answer is "no," there is a silver lining: it means a far more fulfilling career path awaits you. If your answer is "yes," then you now have added and valuable confirmation.

All employees today deserve a caring and highly supportive manager—and that's what they've now come to expect in exchange for their commitment and loyalty at work. This means organizations must choose people for leadership roles who find their greatest fulfillment in making other people win in life—just as Dean Smith did.

In 2023, when she was a research scientist at Harvard University's T.H. Chan School of Public Health and Human Flourishing Program, Dorota Weziak-Bialowolska surveyed over 1,200 employees at a large service company about the psychological climate they experienced at work and analyzed the responses together with data extracted from the employees' health insurance claims and personnel files.[8] Respondents were asked several questions about their organization's psychological and emotional climate of caring, including the extent to which they agreed with statements such as the following:

People feel respected at work.

Employees trust senior leadership.

I feel recognized for my work.

Weziak-Bialowolska's team found that a year after the survey, people who said they experienced more caring leadership were more likely to still be working at the firm, to be more dedicated and productive in their jobs, and to report a greater sense of well-being. Their overall conclusion was that caring managers not only enhance employee well-being, they also drive organizational performance. Their positive influence extends beyond immediate results, creating a thriving and highly productive work environment.

I had my own experience with the power of personally interacting with a leader who I felt truly cared about me as a human being when, less than an hour before I was set to speak to several hundred managers at General Dynamics Information Technology (GDIT) in 2023, I received word that my older brother had unexpectedly died. Because I'd flown nearly three thousand miles to the Washington, DC, area and didn't want to let anyone at the company down on such short notice, I decided to put on a brave face and give the scheduled three presentations before heading home to deal with my loss.

After I successfully made it through my first session, GDIT President Amy Gilliland joined me on stage for a question and answer segment. Her first question to me was, "How are you today, Mark?"

As I'd intentionally buried all of my distress until now and didn't think this was the best moment to disclose my news, I responded by saying, "I'm great, Amy! How are you?"

Perhaps sensing something wasn't right with me, Amy responded with, "How are you *really*, Mark?"

Being asked a second time was the trigger for me to give up the pretense that everything was indeed all right. Doing my best to hold back tears and keep from being overwhelmed by emotion, I told Amy—and everyone else in the auditorium—about my loss.

I'll never forget how warm, generous, and *caring* the GDIT people were to me once they heard my news. And I learned something very important in the process: if you are going to ask someone how they're doing—and you really want to know the answer—ask them how they are, and then follow up by asking how they're *really* doing. It's that word, "really," that tells people you genuinely care about them—and it will help you get to the truth. On any given day, some people will need more support from you than others. You never know in advance which ones.

Final Thoughts

Many years ago, I managed a large region for an American retail bank that was undergoing a truly massive transformation. In order to ensure my team succeeded in making the required changes, I worked countless hours over many months, including most weekends. And I poured every bit of energy and knowledge I had into the job. At the end of the year, my region had triumphed, and I earned a bonus for achieving numerous broad targets.

When my boss handed me my award check, he had a perfect opportunity to praise me, thank me, and acknowledge all of my personal sacrifices.

Instead, he told me he thought my bonus was too large.

Just to be clear, this was not a "you'll never have to work another day in your life" kind of award. At the time, I might have survived a couple of months on those funds. His words were crushing, because I immediately realized he wasn't happy for me or proud of me—he was simply jealous of me. His reaction was a clear sign that he saw me as a competitor rather than being my cheerleader and advocate.

A 2024 Gallup survey found that the percentage of employees who strongly agreed that their organization (and manager) cared about their overall well-being had plunged from 49 percent in 2020 to just 21 percent in 2024.[9]

This precipitous slide, together with the lessons presented in this book, calls for an immediate, monumental shift in our managerial practices and priorities. Bottom line: We need leaders who love their people.

So, spend some time reflecting upon whether or not you truly care about the growth, success, and well-being of *your* people—because that's really what it takes to be an effective manager today.

If you decide that this is who you are, and that this approach to leadership is truly in your blood, oh does the world need you!

CONCLUSION

I think business needs to have a heart,
and to have a heart a company must be more than
just a money-making machine.

—SIR RICHARD BRANSON[1]

My Trip to Oxford

When I was in the final stages of writing this book, I had the opportunity to go to London for a client engagement. On my last day there, I took a train ride out to Oxford University to meet with Jan-Emmanuel De Neve. You'll recall it was his research that proved a direct correlation between employee well-being and team performance—and I genuinely believed it would be a golden opportunity for me to ask him a few last questions face-to-face, and then share the most important insights with you. Here are those insights, and the words of De Neve on which they're based:

Employee well-being is mostly on us (as leaders), not them.

"It used to be that individuals were expected to be responsible for their own well-being. But our research has shown very, very clearly that it's the work environment that greatly influences well-being: Are people paid fairly? Do they feel they belong? Do they have a caring leader? And that's not something the individual employee is responsible for. The whole organization is responsible for this—and the more senior managers are in an organization, the more responsibility they have for it."

Unlike with engagement, a focus on employee well-being is a true win-win.

"What actually matters to people is their well-being. Engagement, on the other hand, is what companies have long sought to get out of people. So, if you think about it, engagement has always been a self-serving and flawed proxy for how people feel.

"There's now a crystallization around this because we're moving ahead into the future of work and, post-COVID, we've really shone a spotlight on employee well-being and mental health directly, rather than what kind of engagement we can get out of people.

"So now, for the first time, the interests of workers and employers are aligned when it comes to supporting well-being."

Measuring well-being should have little complexity.

"In our work, we measure well-being rather basically. My strong recommendation is that leaders do smaller surveys (one to two questions at a time) that capture the essence more often. By using regular pulse surveys, real-time feedback can help you immediately address any issues [rather than] falling behind the curve.

"And, at any given time, we generally want to know two things: how people feel at work, and what may explain those feelings.

"'How happy are you feeling at work?' is our essential question—we used emojis in the British Telecom survey for people to grade themselves and now use an equivalent one to five scale. Then we get into the nitty-gritty of a dozen or so rotating drivers, such as how employees feel about their work-life balance, value and agency, fair pay, whether they have a caring and supportive manager, and health and safety issues. The point is that all of these things, individually, can help explain how people feel better or worse. Knowing how people feel about them lets you more rapidly intervene with remedies whenever they're needed."

Before we parted, I asked Professor De Neve one final question: "What's your most succinct way of conveying to workplace managers the urgency in supporting employee well-being?"

He instinctively replied, "There are really two reasons to buy in. As a human being, you should care about other human beings. And if you don't, you're going to pay for it in finances because your employees will be out the door soon—and retaining people in the future of work will be critical."

My Final Thoughts

By now, I hope you need no further convincing that what people (our employees) need and expect in exchange for their work has been profoundly and inalterably changed in the aftermath of the COVID-19 pandemic—making it essential that we, as leaders, step up, evolve, and purposefully embrace a new managerial mind- and heart-set.

Workplace leadership today demands a much greater understanding and appreciation of humanity—an expanded consciousness of what human beings need in order to flourish—along with a natural desire to support those needs. And while our pivoting in this way is inherently a noble thing to do, we also have the irrefutable clarity that when someone is thriving in their job, they're almost certain to be performing at a high level as well.

As a final piece of punctuation, when you support your employees' well-being in all the ways described in this book, you can fully expect that they will scale mountains for you!

As I say goodbye to you, dear reader, I urge you to channel the wisdom and practices you've encountered here into your daily leadership. Think of Atticus Finch—the central character in Harper Lee's classic novel *To Kill a Mockingbird*—whose quiet strength and steadfast commitment to doing what is right left an indelible mark on his community.

Just as Atticus stood firm in his principles and supported those around him, you too can create a positive impact by prioritizing the well-being of your employees.

By taking immediate action and incorporating these strategies, you have the power to foster a truly thriving workplace. Let us all strive to be the Atticus Finches of our own spheres, leading with empathy, integrity, and a genuine concern for the well-being of others. The time to act is now.

Please Connect with Me!

I welcome the opportunity to remain in contact with you after you return this book to its shelf.

You're invited to connect with me via my website (MarkCCrowley .com) or on LinkedIn or Twitter/X, where I am @MarkCCrowley.

If you email me at Info@MarkCCrowley.com, I'll be happy to send you a long list of leadership books that have influenced my philosophy and were sources for me in writing this book.

I also invite you to listen in to my *Lead from the Heart* podcast (found on my website, Apple podcasts, Spotify, etc.), where I'll introduce you to more inspiring and cutting-edge thinkers who will continue to expand your consciousness—and, of course, your overall leadership effectiveness.

Finally, please go be a positive force, believe deeply in yourself—and love your people. Our world truly aches for visionary, compassionate leaders who will guide us to a brighter future. I very much hope you'll be one of them.

—MCC

THE POWER OF EMPLOYEE WELL-BEING DISCUSSION GUIDE

To facilitate insightful team conversations around the key learnings presented in this book, I have provided a variety of questions related to each chapter. Meeting facilitators—and participants—are encouraged to select the questions they believe will resonate most with their groups.

It's my great hope that these questions will help spark thoughtful dialogue, encourage personal reflections, and, most importantly, inspire actionable insights toward cultivating a culture of well-being within your team.

Introduction

1. What are your initial thoughts on the central thesis of the book?

2. How do you define employee well-being, and how does it differ from traditional concepts of employee engagement?

3. What impact do insincere employee engagement efforts have on overall workplace morale and productivity?

4. What are some practical steps leaders can take to prioritize well-being in the workplace?

5. In your opinion, what are the potential long-term impacts of focusing on well-being, rather than just engagement, on a company's productivity and success?

6. Can you share any personal experiences or examples where prioritizing well-being led to noticeable improvements in your work environment?

Chapter 1

1. Were you surprised by Daniel Kahneman's research findings, which indicate that workplace managers have the least impact on positively influencing employee happiness and well-being?

2. What do you think are the specific reasons many workers feel this way?

3. Big picture, what are some of the leadership remedies?

Chapter 2

1. How do you define self-awareness in the context of leadership, and why is it critical for effective management?

2. Reflecting on your own experiences, can you recall a time when a leader's lack of self-awareness impacted your team or organization? How did it affect you personally?

3. Discuss the importance of understanding one's personal strengths and limitations. How can this understanding enhance leadership effectiveness?

4. How can identifying and reflecting on formative life experiences, such as childhood events and "crucible moments," shape a leader's approach to managing others?

5. In what ways can a manager's unresolved past experiences or biases unconsciously influence their behavior and interactions in the workplace?

6. How can leaders encourage a culture of self-awareness and continuous improvement within their teams?

7. What are some practical steps leaders can take to ensure they remain self-aware and avoid falling into patterns of self-deception or blame shifting?

Chapter 3

1. Why do you think Tim Cook emphasizes leading with one's values as his most important piece of advice?

2. Reflect on your own values. How do they influence your daily decisions and interactions with others?

3. How can having a well-defined personal credo help leaders make better decisions, especially in high-stress situations?

4. Dr. Eric Potterat mentions four key behaviors of elite performers. Which of these behaviors resonates most with you, and why?

5. What are the benefits of focusing on the three things you can control: attitude, effort, and actions? How can this mindset improve performance and reduce stress?

6. Share your thoughts on the process of creating a personal credo. What challenges might you face, and how can you overcome them to ensure your credo truly reflects your core values and beliefs?

Chapter 4

1. How do you interpret Sir Thomas Aquinas's statement that "most people seem to live according to sense rather than reason"? Do you agree with it?

2. Reflect on Antonio Damasio's claim that emotions largely determine our behavior. Can you think of a situation where your emotions influenced a decision you made?

3. Discuss the idea that feelings and emotions may be responsible for up to 95 percent of our decisions and behavior. How does this perspective shift your view of rational decision-making?

4. How can leaders balance the need for logical reasoning with the recognition of the emotional needs of their employees to create a more supportive and productive work environment?

5. In what ways can a leader's self-awareness and understanding of their own emotions enhance their ability to lead and inspire others effectively?

6. How can managers use the understanding that emotions drive employee commitment, loyalty, and productivity to enhance workplace culture? Discuss the impact of ignoring emotions in the workplace. What are some potential consequences for both employees and organizations as a whole?

Chapter 5

1. Reflect on a time when you found it challenging to manage someone with a very different personality or approach from your own. How did you navigate the situation?

2. Why is it important for leaders to embrace the diversity of backgrounds, experiences, and perspectives among their team members?

3. Why is it essential for leaders to avoid taking things personally in the workplace? How can this mindset help reduce stress and improve relationships?

4. How can practicing self-compassion and extending kindness to others create a more positive and productive work environment?

5. How can leaders develop the skill of shifting perspective and seeing the bigger picture during conflicts to make more informed and empathetic decisions?

Chapter 6

1. How does Brené Brown's quote about connection, love, and belonging resonate with your experiences in the workplace?

2. Reflect on Jan-Emmanuel De Neve's study about the drivers of workplace well-being. Why is a sense of belonging considered the most important factor?

3. Why do you think the decline in having a "best friend" at work has occurred, and what impact does this have on employee well-being?

4. Reflect on Dr. Robert Waldinger's findings about the importance of good relationships for health and happiness. How can leaders foster a sense of community and purpose in their teams?

5. What strategies can leaders use to build trust, diversity, and inclusion within their teams to enhance the sense of belonging?

Chapter 7

1. What did Dr. John Gottman discover about the ratio of positive to negative interactions in healthy relationships, and how can this be applied to workplace management?

2. Why is it important for leaders to recognize that negative emotions have a stronger impact than positive ones? How can this awareness influence their leadership style?

3. What are some specific actions leaders can take to ensure they are a positive force in their team, especially during challenging times?

4. Share your thoughts on the role of resilience in maintaining a positive work environment. How can leaders support their team members in building resilience?

5. What are some ways that leaders can encourage open communication and create a safe space for team members to share their thoughts and feelings?

6. How can leaders measure the impact of their positive interactions on team performance and morale over time?

Chapter 8

1. Why is curiosity considered a vital discipline for long-term leadership success?

2. Reflect on a time when you felt your knowledge or skills had become outdated. How did you adapt to the new information or technology?

3. Discuss the concept of confirmation bias and how it can hinder a leader's ability to embrace new perspectives and information.

4. What strategies can leaders use to cultivate curiosity within their teams and encourage continuous learning?

5. How does actively seeking feedback and diverse viewpoints contribute to a leader's growth and effectiveness?

6. How can taking on new and challenging projects help leaders develop their skills and adapt to a rapidly changing world?

Chapter 9

1. How do you interpret Carl Sagan's statement about the universe not being required to align with human ambition?

2. Reflect on a time when you meticulously planned an event or project, but things did not go as expected. How did you handle the situation?

3. Why do you think humans have such a strong need to feel in control of outcomes, and how does this impact our reactions to uncertainty?

4. How can leaders develop the mindset to accept and embrace uncertainty as an inevitable part of life and leadership?

5. How does the ability to unmake decisions, as discussed by Jeff Bezos, contribute to a leader's effectiveness in navigating uncertainty?

6. Discuss the importance of creating an environment where learning from mistakes is valued. How can this mindset benefit both leaders and their teams?

Chapter 10

1. Why is having control over one's workday important for reducing workplace stress and improving well-being?

2. How does establishing clear goals and expectations set the foundation for effective employee autonomy?

3. Why is trust an essential component of effective leadership, and how can managers build trust within their teams?

4. What role do performance metrics play in supporting self-managing teams, and how can managers effectively share this information?

5. How can offering flexibility in when and where work gets done improve employees' well-being and job satisfaction?

6. Discuss the benefits of regular check-ins between managers and employees. How can these meetings contribute to alignment and support?

7. How does fostering a culture of compassion and caring for others promote both individual and organizational well-being?

Chapter 11

1. How do you interpret Steve Jobs's quote about the importance of teamwork in achieving great things in business?

2. Reflect on Dacher Keltner's findings about the benefits of altruism and cooperation. How can these principles be applied in your workplace?

3. How did Microsoft's "stack ranking" system impact employee morale and teamwork during Steve Ballmer's tenure as CEO?

4. What lessons can be learned from the shift in Microsoft's performance evaluation system under Satya Nadella's leadership?

5. What strategies can managers use to foster a culture of collaboration and mutual support within their teams?

6. Reflect on the idea that cooperation is embedded in human DNA. How can leaders leverage this natural tendency to enhance team performance?

7. What steps can leaders take to celebrate teamwork and reinforce the value of collective achievements over individual accomplishments?

Chapter 12

1. How does John Butler Yeats's quote about happiness and growth resonate with your personal experiences in both life and work?

2. Reflect on a time when receiving constructive feedback led to significant personal or professional growth. How did it impact you?

3. Why do you think many people underestimate their talents and potential for growth? How can leaders help their team members realize their hidden potential and capabilities?

4. Discuss the concept of a "fixed mindset" versus a "growth mindset" as explained by Carol Dweck. How can adopting a growth mindset benefit individuals and organizations?

5. How can managers create a Culture of Growth within their teams, as described by Mary C. Murphy?

6. How can regular coaching sessions, even as brief as thirty minutes, positively impact employee motivation and performance?

Chapter 13

1. Reflect on a leader you have known who demonstrated genuine care for their team. How did their approach impact the team's performance and morale?

2. Why do you think stories about caring sports coaches like Dean Smith resonate so strongly with us, while the idea of workplace managers leading with care (and heart) is often viewed differently?

3. Reflect on Dacher Keltner's insight that power is expressed through advocacy, compassion, respect, and attentiveness. How can leaders incorporate these qualities into their leadership style?

4. How can organizations create a culture that prioritizes caring and supportive leadership?

5. How can leaders shift their managerial practices to prioritize the growth, success, and well-being of their people? What changes can they implement to cultivate a more caring leadership approach?

Conclusion

1. What will you always remember from this book?

2. How has your perspective on employee engagement and well-being changed after reading it?

3. Reflect on Sir Richard Branson's statement about businesses needing a heart. How can this philosophy be applied to your current workplace to enhance employee well-being and performance?

4. What specific steps will you take to implement the insights from this book within your team and/or organization?

5. In what ways has this book changed your view of effective leadership?

NOTES

Introduction

1 David Grossman, "10 Inspiring Quotes from Successful CEOs to Help You Win at Employee Engagement," *leadercommunicator* blog, October 23, 2019, https://www.yourthoughtpartner.com/blog/10-inspiring-quotes -from-successful-ceos-to-help-you-win-at-employee-engagement.

2 Mark C. Crowley, "Gallup's Workplace Jedi on How to Fix Our Employee Engagement Problem," *Fast Company*, June 4, 2013, https:// www.fastcompany.com/3011032/gallups-workplace-jedi-on-how-to-fix-our -employee-engagement-problem.

3 Reward & Employee Benefits Association, "Report: State of the Global Workplace," October 17, 2017, https://reba.global/resource/report-state-of -the-global-workplace.html.

4 In January 2025, Gallup reported that 31 percent of US employees are engaged and 17 percent are actively disengaged. Jim Harter, "U.S. Engagement Sinks to 10-Year Low," Gallup, January 14, 2025, https://www.gallup .com/workplace/654911/employee-engagement-sinks-year-low.aspx.

5 Sociabble Communications Team, "Gallup Has Spoken: Trends to Watch in Their 'State of the Global Workplace 2024' Report," November 27, 2024, https://www.sociabble.com/blog/employee-engagement/gallup-state -global-workplace-report/.

6 Gallup began publishing employee engagement scores in 2000.

7 Jen Fisher, "Workplace Burnout Survey: Burnout without Borders," Deloitte, 2015, https://www2.deloitte.com/us/en/pages/about-deloitte /articles/burnout-survey.html.

8 Emma Burleigh, "Workers Are So Burned Out That Nearly 20% Think of Quitting Every Day," *Fortune*, May 6, 2024, https://fortune.com/2024/05/06 /worker-burnout-thinking-quitting-job-daily/.

9   Littler, *The Littler Annual Employer Survey Report*, May 2024, https://
www.littler.com/sites/default/files/2024_littler_employer_survey_report
.pdf?46qu13qkjbr.

10 Heather Stringer, "Worker Well-Being Is in Demand as Organizational
Culture Shifts," American Psychological Association, January 1, 2023,
https://www.apa.org/monitor/2023/01/trends-worker-well-being.

11 Jen Fisher et al., "As Workforce Well-Being Dips, Leaders Ask: What
Will It Take to Move the Needle?" Deloitte, June 20, 2023, https:
//www2.deloitte.com/us/en/insights/topics/talent/workplace-well
-being-research.html.

12 American Psychological Association, *2023 Work in America Survey*, June
2023, https://www.apa.org/pubs/reports/work-in-america/2023-workplace
-health-well-being.

13 Kim Parker and Juliana Menasce Horowitz, "Majority of Workers Who
Quit a Job in 2021 Cite Low Pay, No Opportunities for Advancement,
Feeling Disrespected," Pew Research Center, March 9, 2022, https://www
.pewresearch.org/short-reads/2022/03/09/majority-of-workers-who-quit
-a-job-in-2021-cite-low-pay-no-opportunities-for-advancement-feeling
-disrespected/.

14 Jan-Emmanuel De Neve and George Ward, *Why Workplace Wellbeing Matters: The Science behind Employee Happiness and Organizational Performance*
(Boston: Harvard Business Review Press, 2025).

15 "The Business Case for Wellbeing at Work," posted by World Wellbeing
Movement, YouTube video, December 5, 2023, https://www.youtube.com
/watch?v=t7ZqJc2VIbY.

16 Clément S. Bellet, Jan-Emmanuel De Neve, and George Ward, *Does
Employee Happiness Have an Impact on Productivity?* CEP Discussion Paper
no. 1655, February 2020, https://cep.lse.ac.uk/pubs/download/dp1655.pdf.

17 Jan-Emmanuel De Neve, Micah Kaats, and George Ward, *Workplace Well-
being and Firm Performance*, University of Oxford Wellbeing Research Cen-
tre Working Paper 2304, July 2024, https://doi.org/10.5287/ora-bpkbjayvk.

18 Gurdeep Singh, Milan, and Rashid Zama, "Investigating the Relationship
between Employee Well-Being and Organizational Performance," *Interna-
tional Journal of Research Publication and Reviews* 5, no. 6 (2024): 4472–77,
https://ijrpr.com/uploads/V5ISSUE6/IJRPR30274.pdf.

19 Lisa Monroe, "The Clear Financial Returns on Investing in Employee Well-being," Worklife Digital, February 15, 2024, https://www.worklife.digital/insights/library/the-clear-financial-returns-on-investing-in-employee-wellbeing.

20 Christian Krekel, George Ward, and Jan-Emmanuel De Neve, "Employee Well-Being, Productivity, and Firm Performance: Evidence and Case Studies," in *Global Happiness and Wellbeing: Policy Report 2019*, ed. Jeffrey D. Sachs et al. (Sustainable Development Solutions Network, 2019), 72–93, https://www.hbs.edu/ris/Publication%20Files/gh19_ch5_9e171d71-db54-4e08-a2eb-3cf1587daf4a.pdf.

21 The Conversation and Stephen Bevan, "4 Reasons Why Workplace Wellness Efforts Fail," *Fast Company*, June 23, 2021, https://www.fastcompany.com/90649089/4-reasons-why-workplace-wellness-efforts-fail.

22 William J. Fleming, "Employee Well-Being Outcomes from Individual-Level Mental Health Interventions: Cross-Sectional Evidence from the United Kingdom," *Industrial Relations Journal* 55, no. 2 (2024): 162–82, https://doi.org/10.1111/irj.12418.

23 Fleming, "Employee Well-Being."

24 Julian Hayes II, "Beyond the Paycheck: Why Employees Are Choosing Lifestyle over Salary," *Forbes*, February 24, 2024, https://www.forbes.com/sites/julianhayesii/2024/02/24/beyond-the-paycheck-why-employees-are-choosing-lifestyle-over-salary/.

25 Jim Clifton and Jim Harter, *It's the Manager: Moving from Boss to Coach* (Washington, DC: Gallup Press, 2019).

26 Mark C. Crowley, *Lead from the Heart* podcast, https://www.markccrowley.com/podcasts.

27 Johann Wolfgang von Goethe, *Conversations with Goethe in the Last Years of His Life*, trans. John Oxenford (London: Smith, Elder & Co., 1839).

Chapter 1

1 Apocryphal.

2 Daniel Kahneman et al., "A Survey Method for Characterizing Daily Life Experience: The Day Reconstruction Method," *Science* 306, no. 5702 (2004): 1776–80, https://pdodds.w3.uvm.edu/files/papers/others/everything/kahneman2004a.pdf.

Chapter 2

1 Apocryphal.

2 Tasha Eurich, "Working with People Who Aren't Self-Aware," *Harvard Business Review*, October 19, 2018, https://hbr.org/2018/10/working-with -people-who-arent-self-aware.

3 One guide I've found very useful for identifying one's talents is Marcus Buckingham and Donald O. Clifton's *Now, Discover Your Strengths*, 20th Anniversary ed. (Washington, DC: Gallup Press, 2020).

4 Bill George and Zach Clayton, *True North: Leading Authentically in Today's Workplace, Emerging Leader Edition* (Hoboken, NJ: Wiley, 2022).

Chapter 3

1 "Apple's Tim Cook Gives Commencement Speech at Gallaudet University," posted by Reuters, YouTube video, 1:05:19, May 13, 2022, https:// www.youtube.com/watch?v=d5O7NjLWgeg.

2 Eric Potterat and Alan Eagle, *Earned Excellence: Mental Disciplines for Leading and Winning from the World's Top Performers* (New York: Harper-Collins, 2024).

3 Eric Potterat, interview by Mark C. Crowley, *Lead from the Heart* podcast, "Eric Potterat: The Mental Disciplines for Leading & Winning," February 9, 2024, https://markccrowley.com/eric-potterat-the-mental-disciplines -for-leading-winning/.

4 Rolf Dobelli, *The Art of the Good Life: 52 Surprising Shortcuts to Happiness, Wealth, and Success* (New York: Balance, 2017).

5 Eric Potterat, interview by Mark C. Crowley.

6 Eric Potterat, interview by Mark C. Crowley.

Chapter 4

1 Thomas Aquinas, *Summa Theologica*, I-II, q. 3, a. 3, trans. Fathers of the English Dominican Province (New York: Benziger Brothers, 1947). In this era, the use of the word "men" implied "mankind."

2 Leonard Mlodinow, *Emotional: How Feelings Shape Our Thinking* (New York: Pantheon, 2022).

3 René Descartes, *Discourse on the Method*, trans. Ian Maclean (Oxford: Oxford University Press, 2006).

4 Antonio Damasio, *Descartes' Error: Emotion, Reason, and the Human Brain* (New York: G.P. Putnam's Sons, 1994).

5 Mlodinow, *Emotional*.

6 Zoe Chance, *Influence Is Your Superpower: The Science of Winning Hearts, Sparking Change, and Making Good Things Happen* (New York: Random House, 2022).

7 Marc Brackett, interview by Mark C. Crowley, *Lead from the Heart* podcast, "Marc Brackett: Yale's Chief Emotion Scientist Unlocks Your leadership Potential," September 27, 2019, https://markccrowley.com/marc-brackett -yales-chief-emotion-scientist-unlocks-your-leadership-potential/.

8 Sigal Barsade, interview by Freda Klotz, "Employee Emotions Aren't Noise, They're Data," November 6, 2019, https://sloanreview.mit.edu/article /employee-emotions-arent-noise-theyre-data/.

9 Sigal Barsade, interview by Mark C. Crowley, *Lead from the Heart* podcast, "Sigal Barsade: What's Love Got to Do with Leadership?" August 14, 2020, https://markccrowley.com/sigal-barsade-whats-love-got-to-do-with -leadership/.

10 Julia DiGangi, *Energy Rising: The Neuroscience of Leading with Emotional Power* (Carlsbad, CA: Hay House, 2023).

11 Marc Brackett, *Permission to Feel: Unlocking the Power of Emotions to Help Our Kids, Ourselves, and Our Society Thrive* (New York: Celadon Books, 2019).

12 Quoted in *Maya Angelou: The Complete Collected Poems*, ed. Maria Callahan (New York: Random House, 2005). Angelou is believed to have been paraphrasing Carl W. Buehner, who similarly remarked, "They may forget what you said—but they will never forget how you made them feel" (Richard Evans, ed., *Richard Evans' Quote Book* [New York: Publisher's Press, 1971]).

Chapter 5

1 Alain de Botton, "Why You Will Marry the Wrong Person," *New York Times*, May 28, 2016, https://www.nytimes.com/2016/05/29/opinion /sunday/why-you-will-marry-the-wrong-person.html.

2 R. Matthew Montoya, Robert S. Horton, and Jeffrey Kirchner, "Is Actual Similarity Necessary for Attraction? A Meta-Analysis of Actual and Perceived Similarity," *Journal of Social and Personal Relationships* 25, no. 6 (2008): 889–922, https://doi.org/10.1177/0265407508096700.

3 Brendan Lynch, "Study Finds Our Desire for 'Like-Minded Others' Is Hard-Wired," University of Kansas, February 23, 2016, https://news .ku.edu/news/article/2016/02/19/new-study-finds-our-desire-minded -others-hard-wired-controls-friend-and-partner.

4 Rick Rubin, *The Creative Act: A Way of Being* (New York: Penguin Press, 2023).

5 Naomi Shragai, *The Man Who Mistook His Job for His Life: How to Thrive at Work by Leaving Your Emotional Baggage at Home* (London: W.H. Allen, 2021).

6 Dr. Kristin Neff, *Self-Compassion: Stop Beating Yourself Up and Leave Insecurity Behind* (New York: William Morrow, 2011).

Chapter 6

1 Brené Brown, *Daring Greatly: How the Courage to be Vulnerable Transforms the Way We Live, Love, Parent, and Lead* (New York: Gotham Books, 2012).

2 Emily Rose McRae et al., "9 Trends That Will Shape Work in 2023 and Beyond," *Harvard Business Review*, January 18, 2023, https://hbr.org /2023/01/9-trends-that-will-shape-work-in-2023-and-beyond.

3 Adam Grant, "Friends at Work? Not So Much," *New York Times*, September 4, 2015, https://www.nytimes.com/2015/09/06/opinion/sunday /adam-grant-friends-at-work-not-so-much.html.

4 Alok Patel and Stephanie Plowman, "The Increasing Importance of a Best Friend at Work," Gallup Workplace, January 19, 2024, https://www.gallup .com/workplace/397058/increasing-importance-best-friend-work.aspx.

5 Patel and Plowman, "Increasing Importance".

6 Sara Wachter-Boettcher, "Not Here to Make Friends," Medium, September 13, 2022, https://medium.com/nice-work-from-active-voice/not-here-to -make-friends-c304172d94de .

7 Kritika Langhauser, "HubSpot's 2023 Hybrid Work Report Uncovers Connection as Key Theme Driving the Future of Work," HubSpot, January 30, 2023, https://www.hubspot.com/company-news/2023-hybrid-work-report.

8 Federal Reserve Bank of Philadelphia, "How Time Spent Alone in the US Has Changed over the Past Two Decades—and Implications for Well -Being," October 2, 2022, https://www.philadelphiafed.org/the-economy /macroeconomics/how-time-spent-alone-in-the-us-has-changed-over-the -past-two-decades-and-implications-for-well-being.

9 Joseph Carroll, "Americans Satisfied with Number of Friends, Closeness of Friendships," Gallup, March 5, 2004, https://news.gallup.com/poll /10891/americans-satisfied-number-friends-closeness-friendships.aspx.

10 Daniel A. Cox, "The State of American Friendship: Change, Challenges, and Loss," Survey Center on American Life, June 8, 2021, https://www .americansurveycenter.org/research/the-state-of-american-friendship -change-challenges-and-loss/.

11 US Department of Health and Human Services, *Our Epidemic of Loneliness and Isolation: The US Surgeon General's Advisory on the Healing Effects of Social Connection and Community*, 2023, https://www.hhs.gov/sites/default /files/surgeon-general-social-connection-advisory.pdf.

12 Jamie Ducharme, "America Has Reached Peak Therapy. Why Is Our Mental Health Getting Worse?" *Time*, November 22, 2024, https://time .com/6308096/therapy-mental-health-worse-us/.

13 Robert Waldinger and Marc Schulz, *The Good Life: Lessons from the World's Longest Scientific Study of Happiness* (New York: Simon & Schuster, 2023).

14 Robert Waldinger, interview by Mark C. Crowley, *Lead from the Heart* podcast, "Dr. Robert Waldinger: How to Have a Happy and Fulfilling Life," July 28, 2023, https://markccrowley.com/dr-robert-waldinger-how-to -have-a-happy-and-fulfilling-life/.

15 Grant, "Friends at Work?"

16 Herminia Ibarra, *Act Like a Leader; Think Like a Leader* (Boston: Harvard Business Review Press, 2015).

17 Herminia Ibarra, interview by Mark C. Crowley, *Lead from the Heart* podcast, "Herminia Ibarra: Act before You Think," December 29, 2023, https://markccrowley.com/herminia-ibarra-act-before-you-think/.

18 Jan-Emmanuel De Neve and George Ward, *Why Workplace Wellbeing Matters: The Science Behind Employee Happiness and Organizational Performance* (Boston: Harvard Business Review Press, 2025).

19 Jan-Emmanuel De Neve, interview by Mark C. Crowley, *Lead from the Heart* podcast, "Jan-Emmanuel De Neve: Transform Your Employees' Performance by Prioritizing Their Well-Being," March 21, 2025, https:// markccrowley.com/jan-emmanuel-de-neve-transform-your-employees -performance-by-prioritizing-their-well-being/.

20 Geoffrey L. Cohen, *Belonging: The Science of Creating Connection and Bridging Divides* (New York: W.W. Norton & Company, 2022).

21 Shawn Achor, *The Happiness Advantage: How a Positive Brain Fuels Success in Work and Life* (New York: Crown Currency, 2018).

22 Robert N. Bellah, "Durkheim and Ritual," in *The Cambridge Companion to Durkheim*, ed. Jeffrey C. Alexander and Philip Smith (Cambridge: Cambridge University Press, 2008), 183–210.

23 Michael Norton, interview by Mark C. Crowley, *Lead from the Heart* podcast, "Michael Norton: How Rituals Can Transform Your Team's Connection, Happiness & Performance," May 3, 2024, https://markccrowley.com /michael-norton-how-rituals-can-transform-your-teams-connection -happiness-performance/. Norton is the author of *The Ritual Effect: From Habit to Ritual, Harness the Surprising Power of Everyday Actions* (New York: Scribner, 2024).

Chapter 7

1 Barbara Fredrickson, *Positivity: Top-Notch Research Reveals the Upward Spiral That Will Change Your Life* (New York: Crown Archetype, 2009).

2 John Gottman and Nan Silver, *The Seven Principles for Making Marriage Work: A Practical Guide from the Country's Foremost Relationship Expert* (New York: Harmony Books, 1999).

3 Kyle Benson, "The Magic Relationship Ratio, According to Science," The Gottman Institute, October 4, 2017, https://www.gottman.com/blog/the -magic-relationship-ratio-according-science/.

4 Marcial Losada and Emily Heaphy, "The Role of Positivity and Connectivity in the Performance of Business Teams: A Nonlinear Dynamics Model," *American Behavioral Scientist* 47, no. 6 (2004): 740–65, http://dx.doi.org /10.1177/0002764203260208.

5 Barbara Fredrickson, interview by author, January 2015.

6 Barbara Fredrickson, interview by author, January 2015.

7 John Tierney and Roy F. Baumeister, *The Power of Bad: How the Negativity Effect Rules Us and How We Can Rule It* (New York: Penguin Press, 2019).

Chapter 8

1 John Naisbitt and Patricia Aburdene, *Re-Inventing the Corporation: Transforming Your Job and Your Company for the New Information Society* (New York: Warner Books, 1985).

2 Emily Boudreau, "A Curious Mind: How Educators and Parents Can Encourage and Guide Children's Natural Curiosity—in the Classroom and at Home," Harvard Graduate School of Education, November 24, 2020, https://www.gse.harvard.edu/ideas/usable-knowledge/20/11/curious-mind.

3 Todd B. Kashdan et al., "The Five Dimensions of Curiosity," *Harvard Business Review*, September–October 2018, https://hbr.org/2018/09/the-five-dimensions-of-curiosity.

4 Gary Hamel and Michele Zanini, *Humanocracy: Creating Organizations as Amazing as the People Inside Them* (Boston: Harvard Business Review Press, 2020).

5 Francis Bacon, *Novum Organum* (*1620*), reprinted in E. A. Burtt, ed., *The English Philosophers from Bacon to Mill* (New York: Random House, 1939).

6 Brian Grazer and Charles Fishman, *A Curious Mind: The Secret to a Bigger Life* (New York: Simon & Schuster, 2015).

7 Ben Cohen, "Tim Cook on Why Apple's Huge Bets Will Pay Off," *WSJ Magazine*, October 20, 2024, https://www.wsj.com/style/tim-cook-interview-apple-intelligence-vision-pro-48c59018.

8 Nilofer Merchant, *The Power of Onlyness: Make Your Ideas Mighty Enough to Dent the World* (New York: Viking, 2017).

9 Rick Rubin, *The Creative Act: A Way of Being* (New York: Penguin Press, 2023).

10 Herminia Ibarra, interview by Mark C. Crowley, *Lead from the Heart* podcast, "Herminia Ibarra: Act before You Think," December 29, 2023, https://markccrowley.com/herminia-ibarra-act-before-you-think/.

11 Herminia Ibarra, *Act Like a Leader; Think Like a Leader* (Boston: Harvard Business Review Press, 2015).

Chapter 9

1 Carl Sagan, *Cosmos: A Personal Voyage*, episode 8, "Journeys in Space and Time," directed by Adrian Malone, aired November 9, 1980, on PBS.

2 Rick Wartzman and Kelly Tang, "The Key to Being a Successful Leader? It's Adaptability," *Wall Street Journal*, March 26, 2020, https://www.wsj.com/articles/the-key-to-being-a-successful-leader-its-adaptability-11585242768.

3 Wartzman and Tang, "Key to Being."

4 Jeff Bezos, CEO Letter to Shareholders, Amazon SEC Filing, November 29, 2015, https://www.sec.gov/Archives/edgar/data/1018724 /000119312516530910/d168744dex991.htm.

5 Pico Iyer and Elizabeth Gilbert, "The Future of Hope 3," *On Being* by Krista Tippett, podcast, February 11, 2021, https://onbeing.org/programs /pico-iyer-and-elizabeth-gilbert-the-future-of-hope-3.

Chapter 10

1 Laszlo Bock, *Work Rules!: Insights from Inside Google That Will Transform How You Live and Lead* (New York: Twelve, 2015).

2 William Shakespeare, *King Henry IV, Part Two*, act III, sc. 1.

3 M.G. Marmot et al., "Health Inequalities among British Civil Servants: The Whitehall II Study," *The Lancet* 337, no. 8754 (1991): 1387–93, https:// doi.org/10.1016/0140-6736(91)93068-K.

4 *Stress: Portrait of a Killer*, directed by John Heminway, aired on PBS, April 30, 2008.

5 Gary Hamel, "First, Let's Fire All the Managers," *Harvard Business Review*, December 2011, https://hbr.org/2011/12/first-lets-fire-all-the-managers.

6 Marcus Buckingham and Ashley Goodall, *Nine Lies about Work: A Free-thinking Leader's Guide to the Real World* (Boston: Harvard Business Review Press, 2019).

Chapter 11

1 Steve Jobs, *Steve Jobs: His Own Words and Wisdom* (Cupertino, CA: Silicon Valley Press, 2011).

2 Dacher Keltner, *Born to Be Good: The Science of a Meaningful Life* (New York: W.W. Norton & Company, 2009).

3 Kurt Eichenwald, "Microsoft's Downfall: Inside the Executive E-mails and Cannibalistic Culture That Felled a Tech Giant," *Vanity Fair*, July 3, 2012, https://www.vanityfair.com/news/2012/07/microsoft-downfall-emails -steve-ballmer. Jack Welch famously used a similar methodology later referred to by General Electric employees as "rank and yank." See Jennifer Post, "The End of Rank and Yank: Management Practices Revisited," Business.com, December 19, 2024, https://www.business.com/articles /the-end-of-rank-and-yank-management-practices-revisited/.

4 Eichenwald, "Microsoft's Downfall".

5 Rosabeth Moss Kanter, *Confidence: How Winning Streaks and Losing Streaks Begin and End* (New York: Crown Business, 2004).

6 Daniel Coyle, *The Culture Code: The Secrets of Highly Effective Groups* (New York: Bantam, 2018).

7 Coyle, *The Culture Code.*

Chapter 12

1 John Butler Yeats, *Letters to His Son W. B. Yeats and Others 1869–1922*, ed. Joseph Hone (New York: Macmillan, 1946).

2 William James and Henry James (ed.), *The Letters of William James*, vol. II (Boston: Atlantic Monthly Press, 1920).

3 Biography.com editors and Adrienne Donica, "Rosalynn Carter," November 20, 2023, https://www.biography.com/history-culture/rosalynn -carter#quotes.

4 Carol Dweck, *Mindset: The New Psychology of Success* (New York: Random House, 2006).

5 Mary C. Murphy, *Cultures of Growth: How the New Science of Mindset Can Transform Individuals, Teams, and Organizations* (New York: Simon and Schuster, 2024).

6 Murphy, *Cultures of Growth.*

7 Mark C. Crowley, "Millennials Don't Want Fun; They Want You to Lead Better," LinkedIn Pulse, May 31, 2016, https://www.linkedin.com/pulse /millennials-dont-want-fun-you-lead-better-mark-c-crowley/.

8 Daniel Goleman, "Leadership That Gets Results," *Harvard Business Review* 78, no. 2 (2000): 78–90, https://hbr.org/2000/03/leadership-that-gets-results.

9 Herminia Ibarra, interview by Mark C. Crowley, *Lead from the Heart* podcast, "Herminia Ibarra: Act before You Think," December 29, 2024, https://markccrowley.com/herminia-ibarra-act-before-you-think/.

10 Marcus Buckingham and Ashley Goodall, *Nine Lies about Work: A Free-thinking Leader's Guide to the Real World* (Boston: Harvard Business Review Press, 2019).

11 Marcus Buckingham, interview by Mark C. Crowley, *Lead from the Heart* podcast, "Marcus Buckingham: Why Love and Work Are Inextricable,"

April 7, 2022, https://markccrowley.com/marcus-buckingham-why
-love-and-work-are-inextricable/.

12 Michael Bungay Stanier, *The Coaching Habit: Say Less, Ask More & Change the Way You Lead Forever* (Toronto: Box of Crayons Press, 2016).

13 David Yeager, *10 to 25: The Science of Motivating Young People* (New York: Simon & Schuster, 2024).

14 Liz Wiseman with Greg McKeown, *Multipliers: How the Best Leaders Make Everyone Smarter* (New York: HarperBusiness, 2017).

15 William Shakespeare, *The Tragedy of Hamlet, Prince of Denmark*, act IV, sc. 5.

Chapter 13

1 Dean Smith and Gerald D. Bell, *The Carolina Way: Leadership Lessons from a Life in Coaching* (New York: Penguin Books, 2005).

2 Michael Levy, "Dean Smith: American Coach," *Encyclopedia Britannica*, accessed March 7, 2025, https://www.britannica.com/biography/Dean-Smith.

3 Kathleen Elkins, "10 Life Lessons from Legendary North Carolina Basketball Coach Dean Smith," *The State Journal-Register*, February 9, 2015, https://eu.sj-r.com/story/business/2015/02/09/10-life-lessons-from-legendary/35248464007/.

4 Dacher Keltner, *The Power Paradox: How We Gain and Lose Influence* (New York: Penguin Books, 2017).

5 Austin Suellentrop and E. Beth Bauman, "How Influential Is a Good Manager?" Gallup, June 2, 2021, https://www.gallup.com/cliftonstrengths/en/350423/influential-good-manager.aspx.

6 Unt System Human Resources, "My Supervisor, or Someone at Work, Seems to Care about Me as a Person," undated, https://hr.untsystem.edu/sites/default/files/q5_summary.pdf.

7 Friedrich Nietzche and Daniel Pellerin, *Schopenhauer as Educator: Nietzche's Third Untimely Meditation* (CreateSpace Independent Publishing, 2014).

8 Dorota Weziak-Bialowolska et al., "Psychological Caring Climate at Work, Mental Health, Well-Being and Work-Related Outcomes: Evidence from a Longitudinal Study and Health Insurance Data," *Social Science & Medicine* 323 (2023): 115841, https://doi.org/10.1016/j.socscimed.2023.115841.

9 Maren Gube, Cynthia Matthieu, and Debra Sabatini Hennelly, "How 'Care-washing' Alienates Employees," *Harvard Business Review*, June 10, 2024, https://hbr.org/2024/06/how-carewashing-alienates-employees.

Conclusion

1 Todd Miller, "Screw Business as Usual: An Interview with Sir Richard Branson," SFGate blog, January 9, 2012, https://blog.sfgate.com/tmiller/2012/01/09/screw-business-as-usual-an-interview-with-sir-richard-branson/.

ACKNOWLEDGMENTS

This book is dedicated to the cherished memory of my mother, Irene Jeanne Prioleau Crowley—who died when I was nine years old—and to Carolyn Whitman, who unofficially adopted me, made me part of her family, and loved me all the way until her death at age 95 in 2024.

It's also dedicated to Elizabeth and William Malone, Karlene and John von Szeliski, and Dr. James Casey—all of whom were profoundly supportive, loving, and generous to me at times in my life when I needed them most.

From the moment of conception to the moment of completion, this book surprisingly flowed out of me. As it turned out, I finished the first draft with only a small circle of people even being aware of my project. But those who did know what I was up to proved to have an outsized role in helping me shape it.

My dear friend Ken Boynton didn't just edit the manuscript before I submitted it to my publisher, he was my ongoing sounding board and advisor. For nearly fifteen years, Ken has routinely reassured me of the power of my message, kept me buoyant, and done countless things to support me simply because he deeply believes in me. I'm extraordinarily lucky to have a friend like this.

Kerri Finnecy has been my coach and confidante for nearly two decades. When I first told her that I had an idea for a book and wondered if I should pursue it, she instantly said, "You have to write it—the inspiration you received is a gift from the universe!" I trusted her on that, of course, and consider her one of the greatest blessings in my entire life.

My very, very great friend Scott Davis has purposely been the first person to read all three of my books—including this one. Every time he's read a draft chapter, he's held me to an extremely high standard with his feedback—specifically because he's always believed, and routinely encouraged me to believe, I could meet it.

When I submitted my high-level book proposal to Steve Piersanti, founder and long-time CEO of Berrett-Koehler Publishers, he expressed interest in just a few hours. From that moment forward, his meticulous nature ensured the book I wrote was highly focused and timely. Another gift from the universe, Steve operates with only one goal in mind: excellence. He once told me his company receives fifteen hundred book proposals a year but publishes only thirty to forty of them. It is an immense honor for me to be one of these authors, and to have been so wonderfully supported by Steve and his amazing team. I am deeply grateful to the entire team at Berrett-Koehler for their unwavering support in bringing this book to life. While it's impossible to name every person who contributed to its success, I want to express my heartfelt appreciation for the collective dedication, creativity, and expertise of everyone involved.

A few individuals left an indelible mark on this project. My copy editor, Rachel Head, brought an extraordinary level of care and precision to the manuscript, ensuring every detail was polished with remarkable skill. Ashley Ingram, my collaborator on the cover design, crafted a visual that beautifully captures the essence of the book's themes with inspiration and artistry. And Christy Kirk, whose passion and commitment to marketing and promoting this book made me feel like it was the heart of Berrett-Koehler's mission.

Thank you all for your invaluable contributions to this journey.

While reading Rick Rubin's masterpiece, *The Creative Act: A Way of Being*, I was struck by his observation that human beings possess an "antenna" that picks up on creative ideas circling around in the ether (e.g., to compose a song, paint a picture, write a book, etc.), and it's up to us to acknowledge the inspiration when we receive it and bring it to life.

Rubin's most remarkable insight—which pierced me when I read it—is that any creative idea we receive will inevitably be given to someone else if we fail to bring it into the world—*not because the universe wants to punish us, but because the time for the idea to manifest has come.*

Right before I read that passage, I was still on the fence as to whether or not I wanted to commit to a new writing project. Immediately after I read it, however, I literally said out loud, "Please don't give this book to anyone else! I'm in! I'm your man!" Thank you for the nudge, Rick Rubin.

She won't think it's a big deal, but Felicia Sinusas not only introduced me to Steve Piersanti and Berrett-Koehler, she also helped me get the attention of Hay House, which published my first book. I'll be forever grateful for Felicia's incredibly generous support and thoughtful matchmaking!

My respect and appreciation go to Jan-Emmanuel De Neve, whose remarkable and timely research on well-being confirmed so much of this book's information in unique and highly helpful ways.

Over the years, I have made countless friends around the world through Twitter/X, LinkedIn, Facebook, and my *Lead from the Heart* podcast, and I want to express my deepest and most sincere gratitude to them for supporting me and my work. I can't be more emphatic: if you are one of these many friends, your unwavering advocacy has truly sustained me and kept me motivated to continue creating. Thank you from the bottom of my heart.

I want to thank my family, who sacrificed seeing me often during the months I spent writing. My son Ryan, his wife Rachel, and their three beautiful children, Lauren, Ava, and Anthony, comprise one of the most creative and beautiful families I know. Their love elevates me.

I've also been heartened by the support and encouragement I've long received from my sisters-in-law, Patricia Way and Nancy Casey-Jones, and my brothers-in-law, Steve Way and Wayne Jones. Right before I finished my manuscript, Steve suddenly passed away. I lost a true brother that day and would like to believe he had a hand in ensuring I completed it.

Candy, Paul, Corey, Debbie, and Chip Whitman have been wonderful life-long friends to me. Dear brothers and sisters they truly are—and they encouraged me through every step in writing this book.

I'm profoundly grateful to Marshall Goldsmith for his incisive and wonderfully written foreword, and to Dan Cable, Sally Helgesen, Herminia Ibarra, Hubert Joly, Rhonda Morris, Bob Sutton, and Allison Taylor, who all took the time to read the entire manuscript before crafting beautiful testimonials. Thank you, thank you, thank you!

And finally, I dedicated both editions of my first book, *Lead from the Heart*, to my wife Carol, and the truth is she is truly deserving of having this one dedicated to her as well. No one on the planet has continuously expressed a deeper belief in my work, or has provided more love and nurturing to enable to me to do it. My journey is actually one we've long been on together—and, just like all the people I've already mentioned here, she too is a godsend.

INDEX

George, Bill, 20
Gilliland, Amy, 88–89
Global Council for Happiness and
  Wellbeing, 7
goals, communicating clear, 67
Goldsmith, Dr. Marshall, viii
Goleman, Daniel, 82
Goodall, Ashley, 68, 82
*The Good Life: Lessons from the
  World's Longest Scientific Study of
  Happiness* (Waldinger), 42
Google, 3, 56–57
Gottman, Dr. John, 47, 48, 99
Grant, Adam, 42
Grazer, Brian, 55
Great Resignation, 4
growth mindset, 12, 80–81, 102
growth, personal
  allowing time for, 32
  in business culture, 15
  coaching/mentoring for, 82
  via curiosity, 54, 55
  via doing new things, 57
  encouragement of, 78, 80
  and happiness, 15, 77, 102
  and realizing your potential,
    78–79, 102
  and self-knowledge, 17–18
  underestimating capacity for, 78

H
Hamel, Gary, 54
Hannan, Michael, 74
The Happiness Advantage (Achor), 44
happiness at work
  belonging and, 5–6
  and compassion/empathy,
    66–67
  as employee priority, 32

ideal ratio for, 49
key drivers of, 42–43
and manager relations, 86
and personal growth, 15,
  77, 102
productivity and, 6
and realizing your potential, 80
surveys of, 4–5, 6, 92
Harter, Jim, 8
Harvard Medical School, 42
Harvard University, 88
health, employee
  and agency, 66
  and compassion/empathy,
    66–67
  flexible accounting for, 14–15
  and hierarchical position, 66
  positive emotions and, 48
high-stress situations, 23
Hogan, Kathleen, 73
HR (human resources), 3
HubSpot, 40–41
humanity, embracing shared
  and acceptance of
    disappointment, 60
  and allowing messiness, 35,
    36, 38
  and belonging, 39
  and compassion/empathy,
    36–37
  as leadership best practice, 93
  and navigating conflict, 36, 37
  and need for social rewards, 83
  and self-knowledge, 17–18
  and values-based leadership,
    13, 25
humility, 86
hybrid work, 40, 41
Hybrid Work Report, 41

business culture at, 5
collaboration culture at, 74
commitment to engagement
   by, 3
employee sabotage of, 1
growth mindset of, 81
heart of, 91
problems facing many, 3
role of emotions in, 31
stress and position in, 65
success of, viii, 1
well-being commitments of, 4, 7
Oxford University, 4, 7, 42, 91

P

pain, emotional, 32
parental influences, 19, 20
Patagonia, 3
perfectionism, 20
performance
   in high-stress situations, 23–24
   learned behaviors for elite, 24
   non-elite, 25
performance, employee
   and belonging, 39–40, 44
   and care from managers, 86
   and ceding of managerial
      control, 67
   and competitiveness, 71–74
   on cooperative teams, 71, 75
   and emotions, 13, 31
   encouraging growth in, 79–80
   and engagement, 2
   expectations of, 32
   manager behavior and, 8, 63
   positive interactions and, 48, 49
   routine measures of, 68
   stack ranking of, 72–73

weekly check-ins about, 68
and well-being, 91, 93
*Permission to Feel: Unlocking the
Power of Emotions to Help Our
Kids, Ourselves, and Our Society
Thrive* (Brackett), 31
personality traits, 36
Plato, 29, 30
podcasts, listening to new, 58
positive interactions
   growth as encouraged in, 78
   how to increase, 14, 51
   ideal ratio for, 47, 49–50, 99
   and leadership expertise, 48
   with managers, 33, 50
potential, realizing your, 78–79
Potterat, Dr. Eric, 23, 25, 26
power
   and care, 86
   and positive emotions, 32
*The Power of Bad: How the
Negativity Effect Rules Us and How
We Can Rule It* (Baumeister and
Tierney), 49
The Power of Employee Well-Being
   (Crowley), vii, viii
The Power of Onlyness (Merchant), 56
*The Power Paradox: How We Gain
and Lose Influence* (Keltner), 86
praise/appreciation, 48
productivity
   and belonging, 42, 44
   of cooperative teams, 71, 74, 75
   via employee empowerment, 69
   employee engagement and, 2
   encouraging growth in, 79–80
   well-being as driver of, vii, 6–7,
      8, 93

professional development, 5
psychological/emotional needs, 3
purpose at work, 5

Q

quality of life, 7
quitting work
    daily thoughts of, 3
    Great Resignation, 4

R

rationality, emotions and, 29–30, 37
Reid, Andy, 74
relationships
    behavior for healthy, 48
    creative building of, 44
    employee/manager, 86
    importance of coworker, 41, 99
    positive interactions in, 47,
      50–51
    self-awareness in, 21
    team cohesion, 39–40
    work friendships, 40–41, 99
remote work, 40, 41
resilience, 24, 50
respect, 19
responsibility
    for employee well-being, 91
    and job stress, 66
    taking personal, 18
retention, employee, 4, 6
rituals, team, 44–45
Rubin, Rick, 36, 56
Rule of Four, 50

S

safety
    and curiosity/listening, 57

    manager's contribution to, 33
    and tolerance, 13
Sagan, Carl, 59, 100
Saïd Business School, 4
Salesforce, 3
sarcasm, 19
"Schopenhauer as Educator"
    (Nietzsche), 87
Schwartz, Robert, 49
self-awareness
    change via, 13, 19
    of crucible moments in life, 20
    and culture of well-being, 95
    in interactions with others,
      20–21
    as lifelong journey, 21
    and life path, 87
    for managers/leaders, 17–18,
      96, 98
    payoff of, 21
    and realizing your potential,
      78–79
self-compassion, 38
self-doubt, 79
self-mastery, 24
setbacks, responding to, 59–60
*The Seven Principles for Making
    Marriage Work* (Gottman), 47
Shakespeare, William, 65, 84
Shragai, Naomi, 37
skills, honing of, 77–78, 82, 84, 102
sleep apps, 7
Smith, Dean, 15, 85–86, 87, 103
social electricity, 44
social pressure, 25
social rewards, 83
solitude, health effects of, 41
stack ranking, 72–73, 102

Stanford University, 43, 80
State of the American Workplace
   study, 1
strengths
   diversity as, 36
   knowing your, 18, 19
   overestimation of, 54
stress
   and employee burnout, 3
   and hierarchical position,
      65–66, 101
   and lack of control, 66
   management classes, 7
   for managers/leaders, 25
success
   via caring for your team, 85,
      90, 103
   via collaboration, 74–75
   via curiosity, 56–57
   via employee well-being, viii, 1
   via growth mindset, 80–81
superiority, illusory, 51
surveys
   of belonging at work, 39–40
   of corporate effectiveness, 61
   of culture of care, 88
   Day Reconstruction Method,
      11–12
   of employee engagement,
      1–2
   employee indifference to, 2
   of employee well-being, 92
   of happiness at work, 42–43
   of job satisfaction factors,
      40–41
   of manager care, 90
   practical applications from, 10
   of workplace stress, 65–66

T

talent, growth of, 77–78, 82, 84, 102
Tang, Kelly, 61
teams
   and belonging, 5
   ceding control to, 67, 69
   cohesion in, 39–40, 42, 44, 45
   competition amidst, 72–74, 102
   cooperative, 15, 71, 73, 74, 102
   culture of well-being for, 95
   curiosity culture on, 56–57
   decision making by small, 63
   defining values for, 45
   as families, 74
   fostering connection for, 13–14
   for new hires, 45
   power of teamwork, 86
   regular check-ins with, 82–83
   rituals/celebrations for, 44–45
   secret to high-performing, 48
   self-reflection on, 75
*10 to 25: The Science of Motivating
   Young People* (Yeager), 83
thriving vs. engagement, vii
Tierney, John, 49
time, preciousness of, vii
To Kill a Mockingbird (Lee), 93
transformation, inner/outer, 13
Triggers (Goldsmith), viii
triggers, understanding your, 21
trust
   and belonging, 5, 99
   and ceding of managerial
      control, 67
   listening to build, 56
   modeling, 25–26
   and teamwork, 75

ABOUT THE AUTHOR

 MARK C. CROWLEY is a visionary leader and best-selling author, renowned for his transformative approach to workplace management and optimizing employee performance. With over twenty-five years of experience in the highly competitive financial services industry, Mark defied traditional leadership norms by consistently demonstrating that the key to unlocking human potential lies in emotional connection and genuine care.

From his early days as a management trainee to his two national-level roles at one of America's largest financial institutions, Mark's leadership style stood out for its intentional focus on people rather than just numbers. He believed in making employees feel valued, identifying their unique talents, and providing opportunities for their growth. His highly uncommon approach not only led to his teams consistently exceeding performance targets but to him being named his firm's "Leader of the Year."

Mark's philosophy is encapsulated in his bestselling book, *Lead from the Heart: Transformational Leadership for the 21st Century*, which has been taught at eleven American universities to date.

On the vanguard of workplace leadership thinking, Mark directly challenged longstanding managerial practices and proved with irrefutable research that our conventional approach to motivating employee performance is entirely misaligned to human nature—and therefore demands reinvention.

The consistent theme of all of Mark's work is that workplace leaders perform best when they balance mind and heart in their interactions with people—and when they authentically care about them as well. His ideas have resonated with leaders worldwide, inspiring a global movement toward more humane and supportive management practices.

In 2018, Mark launched the *Lead from the Heart* podcast, which has become a platform for world-class authors, innovators, and CEOs to share their insights on leadership and human connection. His podcast has garnered a loyal audience in 175 countries and ranks among the top 1.5 percent of all worldwide podcasts.

As a global speaker and organizational culture consultant, Mark continues to advocate for a leadership style that prioritizes employee well-being. His work has been recognized by *Forbes* magazine as visionary and a blueprint for the future of workplace leadership. His clearly articulated mission is to fundamentally change how we lead and manage people, making our practices far more supportive of human needs.

Mark is a regular contributor to *Fast Company*. His work has been published by *USA Today*, *HuffPost*, *The Seattle Times*, Thrive Global, Reuters, *Stanford Social Innovation Review*, and Gallup. He's a graduate of the University of California, San Diego, and the Pacific Coast Banking School at the University of Washington.

Mark grew up in Garden City, New York, and now lives in La Jolla, California.

Introducing the Berrett-Koehler Community

Support mission-based publishing while saving up to
30 percent on all books and attending exclusive events

Are you passionate about supporting independent
publishing and reading diverse voices and
perspectives?

Join the BK Community Membership Program and
become a part of a vibrant literary community.
Since 1992 we have been discovering and
amplifying the voices of authors who drive positive
change through books that connect people and
ideas to create a world that works for all.

This membership program will help Berrett-Koehler
Publishers thrive financially, broaden and deepen
our global community, spread our mission, and
diversify our revenues for a sustainable future.

Visit ideas.bkconnection.com/bkcommunity-join or scan the QR code
to learn more and become a member.

Berrett–Koehler
Publishers

Berrett-Koehler is an independent publisher dedicated to an ambitious mission: *Connecting people and ideas to create a world that works for all.*

Our publications span many formats, including print, digital, audio, and video. We also offer online resources, training, and gatherings. And we will continue expanding our products and services to advance our mission.

We believe that the solutions to the world's problems will come from all of us, working at all levels: in our society, in our organizations, and in our own lives. Our publications and resources offer pathways to creating a more just, equitable, and sustainable society. They help people make their organizations more humane, democratic, diverse, and effective (and we don't think there's any contradiction there). And they guide people in creating positive change in their own lives and aligning their personal practices with their aspirations for a better world.

And we strive to practice what we preach through what we call "The BK Way." At the core of this approach is *stewardship,* a deep sense of responsibility to administer the company for the benefit of all of our stakeholder groups, including authors, customers, employees, investors, service providers, sales partners, and the communities and environment around us. Everything we do is built around stewardship and our other core values of *quality, partnership, inclusion,* and *sustainability.*

We are grateful to our readers, authors, and other friends who are supporting our mission. We ask you to share with us examples of how BK publications and resources are making a difference in your lives, organizations, and communities at bkconnection.com/impact.

Dear reader,

Thank you for picking up this book and welcome to the worldwide BK community! You're joining a special group of people who have come together to create positive change in their lives, organizations, and communities.

What's BK all about?

Our mission is to connect people and ideas to create a world that works for all.

Why? Our communities, organizations, and lives get bogged down by old paradigms of self-interest, exclusion, hierarchy, and privilege. But we believe that can change. That's why we seek the leading experts on these challenges—and share their actionable ideas with you.

A welcome gift

To help you get started, we'd like to offer you a **free copy** of one of our bestselling ebooks:

bkconnection.com/welcome

When you claim your **free ebook**, you'll also be subscribed to our blog.

Our freshest insights

Access the best new tools and ideas for leaders at all levels on our blog at ideas.bkconnection.com.

Sincerely,

Your friends at Berrett-Koehler